Leaving the Lectern

Leaving the Lectern

*Cooperative Learning and the Critical First
Days of Students Working in Groups*

Dean A. McManus
University of Washington

ANKER PUBLISHING COMPANY, INC.
Bolton, Massachusetts

Leaving the Lectern
Cooperative Learning and the Critical First Days of Students Working in Groups

ISBN 1-882982-85-1

Composition by Jessica Holland
Cover design by Jessica Holland

Anker Publishing Company, Inc.
563 Main Street
P.O. Box 249
Bolton, MA 01740-0249 USA

www.ankerpub.com

Library of Congress Cataloging-in-Publication Data

McManus, Dean A.
Leaving the lectern : cooperative learning and the critical first days of students working in groups / Dean A. McManus.
p. cm.
Includes bibliographical references and index.
ISBN 1-882982-85-1
1. College teaching—Evaluation. 2. Active learning. 3. Group work in education. I. Title.

LB2331.M395 2005
378.1'2—dc22

2004029185

They who set themselves to give precepts must of course regard themselves as possessed of greater skill than those to whom they prescribe; and if they err in the slightest particular, they subject themselves to censure. But as this tract is put forth merely as a history, or, if you will, as a tale, in which, amid some examples worthy of imitation, there will be found, perhaps, as many more which it were advisable not to follow, I hope it will prove useful to some without being hurtful to any, and that my openness will find some favour with all.

—René Descartes, *Discourse on Method*

For each student in my first class of cooperative learning.
If I was a pioneer, then so were you.

As Walt Whitman sang,
"venturing as we go the unknown ways,
Pioneers! O pioneers!"

ABOUT THE AUTHOR

Dean A. McManus is professor emeritus in the School of Oceanography at the University of Washington. He received his B.S. degree in geology from Southern Methodist University in 1954 and his M.S. and Ph.D. degrees in geology from the University of Kansas in 1957 and 1959, respectively. His marine geological research has dealt mainly with sediments on the floor of the Chukchi and Bering seas and off Washington State. He was co–chief scientist on the first cruise in the Pacific Ocean of the drilling vessel *Glomar Challenger* of the National Science Foundation (NSF)-funded Deep-Sea Drilling Project. He has been honored by the National Oceanic and Atmospheric Administration for his marine geological research by having an underwater mountain in the North Pacific Ocean named after him, McManus Seamount. For 23 years he was editor of the research journal *Marine Geology*.

After years of undergraduate teaching by lecture and examination, he changed his teaching method to cooperative learning and project evaluation and by so doing pioneered the use of cooperative learning in the teaching of undergraduate oceanography. As a Distinguished Speaker for the National Association of Geoscience Teachers, he, with one of his students, led workshops on cooperative learning in geoscience departments at several colleges and universities in the United States and Canada. He has also been co-leader of NSF-funded workshops on innovative teaching in the geosciences during summers and at national meetings of the American Geophysical Union (AGU) and the Geological Society of America, and at the Ocean Sciences Meetings of the American Society of Limnology and Oceanography and the AGU.

Dr. McManus has also organized and participated in sessions on innovative geoscience education for these and other scientific societies, especially while serving as a member of the Committee on Education and Human Resources of the AGU. He has often been an invited speaker on geoscience education and has published in the *Journal of Geoscience Education*, the *Journal of College Science Teaching*, and *Geotimes*. He also wrote a column, "In the Oceanography Classroom," for *Oceanography* magazine, the journal of The Oceanography Society. In 2000, he was co-leader of the NSF-sponsored workshop that recommended the NSF establish Centers for Ocean Sciences Education Excellence, which was done in 2002.

At the University of Washington, Dr. McManus has received the Distinguished Undergraduate Teacher Award of the College of Ocean and Fishery Sciences. For two years he served as the first faculty associate in the Center for Instructional Development and Research and developed a New TA Orientation Program that involved teaching workshops for new graduate students in the School of Oceanography, the first such program in an oceanography graduate program. In addition, the Mossfield Foundation established in the School of Oceanography the Dean A. McManus Excellence in Teaching Award to be given annually to an outstanding graduate teaching assistant.

CONTENTS

FOREWORD

What does it take to transform the teaching of science? Anyone who has sat in a classroom listening to a professor drone on interminably recognizes the problem. But how does one move to address it?

"How many psychiatrists does it take to change a light bulb? One, but the light bulb has to want to change." Perhaps the message in the old joke is the correct one: Turning on the light of learning begins with the teacher wanting to change.

Dean McManus shared with me an outline of a story of his own personal odyssey and transformation in teaching, and I encouraged him to share it with others. But then he did something that surprised me; he followed through.

More than seven years later, this emeritus professor of oceanography at the University of Washington has produced a volume to record his transformation from lecturing to guiding, from "professing" to engaging. Professor McManus learned about learning; he also learned to give students responsibility and control of their own learning. And the students moved from listening and writing to experiencing. After all, this is what they'll have to do for the rest of their lives!

This book will reassure its readers that they and their students will survive this transformation in teaching. The book can also support their risk-taking.

Improving undergraduate instruction in the sciences is an important goal. It is likely to be an elusive one as well, until it is valued and expected, and until systems are put in place to educate and support faculty.

The knowledge of "how to teach" is not conferred with the doctorate. It is learned behavior. Professor McManus's students who have gone on to the academy have another and a different model to emulate, and now the wisdom from his practice.

Shirley M. Malcom, Ph.D.
Head, Directorate for Education and Human Resources Programs
American Association for the Advancement of Science (AAAS)

PREFACE

Why a Book?

How many times have you heard it said that college and university faculty ought to change the way we teach so that we can enhance our students' learning? We hear this more often now for the simple reason that more is being discovered about how students learn. And if we know how students learn, goes the reasoning, then why don't we teach them in ways that make use of this knowledge and thereby enhance their learning? After all, as a search for "sports biomechanics" on the web will demonstrate, athletic coaches and teachers use their increased knowledge of how the human body moves so that they can both reduce injury and enhance the performance of students in athletic activities. Therefore, if we do not use the increased knowledge of how students learn so that we can likewise both reduce injury (our boring lectures, paltry expectations for learning, untutored perceptions of student diversity, and mechanical assessment of learning) and enhance the performance of students in learning activities, are we not doing less to enhance student learning than coaches are to enhance student athletic performance? Isn't it the enhancement of student learning, rather than student athletic performance, that should be the primary achievement of higher education?

What it all boils down to is replacing much of our lecturing with learning activities in which students can take an active part, such as talking about the subject in their own words as well as listening to other people's words, and writing about it in their own phrases as well as copying down other people's phrases. It's called active learning, which comes in many formats, one of which—cooperative learning—is the subject of this book. But this replacement goes much deeper than merely changing teaching techniques. And the implications of the change for enhancing the learning of all students are far reaching. For instance, an active learning experience can develop interpersonal relationships among students working in a group, break down stereotypes, and provide support for learning by underrepresented minorities that is all but impossible when, isolated and anonymous, students passively take notes in a lecture class. The critical significance of this particular aspect of learning enhancement is evident in the United States census data that projects minorities to form an ever increasing percentage of the college-age population, attaining a majority in the next 50 years (National Science Foundation, 2004).

Slow as the change in teaching is in higher education, it is conspicuously slow in research universities. Handelsman et al. (2004) note with astonishment that this faculty, though steadfast to evidence in their research, demanding of rigorous proof in research assertions, and bold in exploring new avenues of research, fail to apply these same skills when it comes to teaching. Instead, according to Handelsman et al.—and I agree—they ignore or are unaware of the evidence from research on how people learn, "defend on the basis of the intuition alone teaching methods that are not the most effective" (p. 521), and instead of exploring new avenues of teaching, cling to, what is in effect, the way they were taught.

One might wonder why the reform of undergraduate education should be so important for faculty at research universities, which are only 3% of the institutions of higher education in the country. The answer is simple: Those 3% of the higher education institutions grant one-third of all baccalaureate degrees and just over half the baccalaureate degrees of future Ph.D. holders in science and engineering (Boyer Commission on Educating Undergraduates in the Research University, 1998).

Have you wondered whether—assuming you could ever find the time—you should try to change the way you teach? Or have you already read some directions for making that change (and there are ever so many fine books of directions out there), but didn't see how to apply those directions to yourself and your students? Or have you ever tried to visualize what in the world teaching in this new way would be like, what you would actually do in the classroom, and got nothing but an error message on that virtual screen? Or do you think you are already achieving the goals of enhanced student learning by teaching as you were taught? If you answer "yes" to any of these questions, or are just plain curious about teaching, particularly in research universities, then this book is for you.

My purpose is not to write another book of directions on how to change your teaching, but to show you by my example how someone, perhaps much like you, changed the way he taught undergraduate students. For years I taught the way I had been taught, the way my colleagues taught, the only way I knew how to teach—in fact, the only way I thought anyone could teach a class of 20 to 40 students: by lecture—to provide information—and by examination—to determine whether the students had learned what I had taught them. Teaching, however, was a routine assignment for me, an important—but secondary—part of the job. My main responsibility as a faculty member was to do research, which I enjoyed. After all, I was at a research university, where the emphasis is always on research, and the contributions to knowledge that have come from research at these institutions certainly justify that emphasis.

Then something—and I knew not what—drove me to change my teaching. I put students together to work in groups, and I assessed their learning by the projects they completed. But this change did not happen overnight. And during the change, which never truly ended, I gained both personal satisfaction and professional esteem. The students and I agreed that they had learned more and had enjoyed the learning more than in a lecture class, and that we had all worked our tails off.

Furthermore, I did this in a discipline that does not treat education as the subject of its research. I'm an oceanographer. So I know what it's like to have established yourself as a scholar in your discipline, which has nothing to do with the scholarly discipline of education, and to be highly skilled in the scholarly methods of your discipline, and to be accorded a reasonable level of prestige for your research accomplishments in your discipline, and also to be somewhat accomplished in the skills of teaching your discipline. And I know the anxiety that then grips you when you find yourself in a classroom, trying to teach in a different way, with no guarantee of what will happen next.

The very thought of placing yourself in that situation may churn your stomach. After all, you're accustomed to being an expert learner of knowledge in your discipline. Now you are being asked to bare your ignorance as a novice to learn new skills of teaching without knowing what to expect, and to do all this without being able to visualize your classroom. You may have said, "I don't know what a class emphasizing student learning is supposed to look like or be like" or "I wouldn't know what to do with myself in the classroom if I wasn't lecturing." Even worse, you are being asked to bare your ignorance in front of your students, which is asking a lot. I can imagine your anxiety, "I may make a fool of myself in front of my students" or "I can't turn my lecture notes into student activities" or "Students have never been willing to talk in my classes" or "Students will never participate in group activities."

I believe that an example of how someone else learned these workplace skills may enlighten you in a way that reading or listening to directions for change may not. It's like the difference between reading a cookbook's directions to "stir sauce until thickened" and wondering how thick is "thickened," and watching, through the printed page, a cook stir the sauce until the bottom of the pan is revealed as a track behind the spoon stirring the now-thickened sauce.

This book is about the term in which I changed my course to cooperative learning, with a detailed description of those critical first few days of the term. Although I comment a little on changes I made for the second year, my emphasis is on the term in which I changed the format of the course, for that is the most difficult period. In later years, you will go your own way. Because this book is, in effect, a journal, you'll witness both the achievements and the mistakes, the latter perhaps being more useful to you because witnessing someone else recognize his mistakes is an unforgettable way to learn. And I'll share with you my joy in the enterprise—yes, I said "joy," as in "the joys of teaching" (Eble, 1983, p. 36).

How Should You Use the Book?

As you read how I made each change, either effectively or ineffectively, I'll cite references with detailed information on the assumptions behind the change, directions for making the change, or lists of the learning results to be expected from making the change. Here is where I think this book can be of great service to you.

The literature on teaching and learning in higher education is enormous, surprisingly so to those of us who had never thought about it. Which book on directions for teaching should you pick up? Which directions should you begin with? This book can serve as your guide to entering that literature. The references that I'll cite most often are the two listed most often by teaching centers on their web sites: Barbara Gross Davis's (1993) *Tools for Teaching* and Wilbert J. McKeachie's (2002) *Teaching Tips.* I urge you to begin your change by using one of these books for directions. I shall also cite several books on special aspects of active learning, particularly on the format known as cooperative learning, and several citations will be to web sites that you can access at once.

In the citation to these references, I'll often assist you by giving the topic in the reference, usually a heading or subheading, following the year of publication, for instance, (Davis, 2003, Syllabus), and thus tie my example to the precept. We'll go from the concrete to the abstract, rather than the other way around as in books of directions. These books should be available in your campus library or teaching center. As a further help to you, I have placed reflective questions at the end of each chapter to prepare you to use the information in the chapter.

Most important, I hope you'll be able to use my experience to visualize what teaching in this different manner is like. You can add your own experiences to it. And if you visualize it over and over, it will lose its strangeness. Then, when you change the way you teach, the situation won't be foreign; it "won't scare you" (Covey, 1990, p. 134). To quote Johnson (1998), "When you see how [change] can make things better, you get more interested in making the change happen" (p. 87). Please note, though, that it is not my intent that you should teach exactly as I did. There are many formats of active learning for you to choose from.

What's in the Book?

What will this book cover? Chapter 1 is a sketch of my teaching from the time I arrived as a postdoctoral fellow at a research university until I learned about the various formats of active learning. By drawing on comments from student evaluations and a few notes that I made to myself, I present the teaching environment that I worked in, which many of you may recognize intimately. I'll emphasize the senior-level course that I later changed from lecture and examination to cooperative learning and student projects. But the only change that I thought could be made in my teaching before that was a change in the content, the transfer of content to the students being the sole purpose of teaching, as I understood it. Eventually, though, I got it into my head that I needed to make some other kind of changes in my teaching, and to my surprise those changes became a form of teaching that some people find chaotic, but I find very comfortable, in spite of being a highly structured person. It could happen to you. Those changes do entail some risks, however.

Chapter 2 is about taking risks in the classroom. Let's face it. We do not enjoy taking risks. We are anxious about them (some would say fearful). In fact, fear or anxiety is an unmentioned aspect of being a teacher that I'll discuss. We avoid risks even though we are highly trained risk takers. It is important for you to realize your proven ability to accept calculated risks, for they can help you change your teaching. I'll also discuss six steps that can help you better prepare to make the change.

Chapter 3 emphasizes that you do not have to change your teaching in a course all at once. You can change it piecemeal, an option that should make the change easier to implement. You will learn where to look for telltale signs that you may have already made some changes without realizing the significance of what you were doing. It happened to me, as I'll describe. Each change in itself was insignificant, but in retrospect the sum of the changes revealed an underlying desire to make a major change in my teaching. Even past changes that failed can be valuable clues for building your self-confidence to undertake the challenge.

Chapter 4 begins with questions and ends with answers. Although we ask ourselves questions about our research and seek answers to those questions all the time, we tend not to ask questions, let alone seek answers, about our teaching or our students' learning. We can learn how to begin asking those questions by listening more closely to the questions about teaching and learning that our students ask us. Ironically, the answers to those questions often come from the students themselves. I'll touch on the five ways we can seek answers to students' questions and describe my search for answers. After acquiring the information, I then wanted to share it. That scholar's desire led me to my first education meeting, which happened to be in an active learning format and in my discipline. I'll describe the meeting in detail because what I learned there changed my teaching and my life.

Chapter 5 narrates the two weeks of preparation I undertook to change my course from lecture and examination to cooperative learning and student projects; it also describes the first day of class for the 22 students. I tell how I changed my lecture notes into student reading assignments, what I said and did on the all-important first day of class (and what I failed to do), and why I chose not to grade assignments that were passports to student participation in the class.

Chapter 6 details the second through sixth days of the course. The second day records how the students worked in their first groups—their learning groups—what I did in the classroom, my feelings about what was happening, what I failed to do, and how I continually underestimated the time required for the students to complete their activities. The third and fourth days record their activities in their second groups—their teaching groups—and the fifth and sixth days record their activities in solving problems based on what they had learned the previous two days. My decisions and actions, for better or worse, are also recorded, particularly my panic on falling behind in covering content. In Chapters 5 and 6 there are many citations to references containing directions for the proper use of the methods I applied and to the importance of decisions and actions that I took or failed to take. This book helps you to see how these methods fit into the big picture of teaching and learning.

Since the principal goal of changing the way we teach is to enhance students' learning, we must assess that learning. Chapter 7 begins by recognizing that in order to assess students' learning, we must know what we want students to learn and, more challenging for us, we must express it in such a way that allows us to assess whether they have learned it. This challenge forces us to consider our goals for a course, a task at which I had fallen short for years, and I describe how, by not covering so much content in the course as I had when lecturing, I finally discovered who my students were, at least to the extent that it gave me my first insight into what I wanted them to know when they left the course and what I wanted them to be able to do with that knowledge. And I give some examples of assessments made by the students and by me. I describe the learning significance of three of the projects that I used in place of exams and my rudimentary reflection on grading. I also share my joy in observations that convinced me that students were indeed learning, and my joyless recognition of my shortcomings.

Chapter 8 looks at the other side of the assessment coin—assessing our teaching, a touchy subject for most faculty in the best of times. The goal is to determine how we might further change our teaching to improve our students' learning. Change is an integral part of teaching by active learning methods because the instructor must adapt and exhibit flexibility. I give several examples of adaptation and flexible changes that I made as events occurred in the course. I experienced the truth of the saying "Blessed are the flexible, for they will not be bent out of shape." And, yes, I know the other version, "Blessed are the flexible, for they tie themselves into knots," but that didn't happen to me. The critical ability to make these changes, often unanticipated, is not detected by most tools for assessing teaching, including the three main tools: the end-of-term course evaluation by the students, the Midterm Class Interview, and peer review. I mention the latter two methods, and I describe the students' evaluation of my course—the joy it gave me for daring to risk changing my teaching and the constructive criticism it provided me to improve the course for the future.

The seclusion of the classroom does not make change easy. Chapter 9 discusses how I made connections with other people to inform them about the change in my teaching and to obtain feedback from them. They included colleagues in the department, other faculty on campus, and faculty in my discipline at other institutions. The last-mentioned connections occurred at meetings of professional organizations where education workshops were held and education sessions presented, in the education journals of my discipline, and through guest speaking in my discipline. Education workshops are also held by organizations outside our disciplines. The possibility exists of our going deeper into the subject of teaching and learning either in general or in our discipline.

In Chapter 10, I describe my need to find a frame of reference that would make sense of my teaching, in and out of the classroom. This need led me to discover writings about the teaching-centered and learning-centered paradigms of education, which are the frames of reference. From these writings I came to understand that how I had been teaching before the change was not according to some natural law. It was merely a method to attain educational goals that I had accepted involuntarily. This realization reassured me that the change was right for me. The contrast between these paradigms is more fundamental than teaching methods and explains the basis for our natural resistance to changing from one paradigm to the other. But this resistance can be overcome.

Not only do we change our concepts about education but we also can change our concepts about ourselves as teachers, as explored in Chapter 11. With this change in ourselves, we put aside the four familiar excuses for not changing our teaching. More significant, we begin to discover what gladdens us about teaching. Hokey though the idea may seem to you now, you can begin to discover the teacher within you.

The conclusion brings together the seven themes woven throughout the book, and the appendix provides a sketch of what is driving this national reform of undergraduate education.

Dean A. McManus
Seattle, WA
September 2004

ACKNOWLEDGMENTS

With deep appreciation I acknowledge the following people, who, in chronological order, played key roles in my development as a teacher, in the change in my teaching, and in the writing of this book.

JOE CREAGER, School of Oceanography, University of Washington—for insisting that teaching was the way for me to learn oceanography.

ARTHUR NOWELL, then director, School of Oceanography, University of Washington—for graciously funding my "special class" on Thursdays and my travel to The Meeting.

ANGIE THOMSON-BULLDIS, then a student in my class—for asking me a critical question.

ED BUCHWALD, Department of Geology, Carleton College—for describing a classroom environment that was new and exciting to me.

BARBARA TEWKSBURY, Department of Geology, Hamilton College—for a five-page handout that changed my teaching and my life and for an invitation to be a distinguished speaker and a co-leader of workshops on innovative teaching.

JANICE DeCOSMO, Washington NASA Space Grant Consortium—for attending my brown-bag lunch talk and being my first connection to innovative teaching on campus.

CAROL KUBOTA, Education Program, University of Washington–Bothell—for professionally encouraging me to be a "pioneer" in innovative teaching.

HEATHER MACDONALD, Department of Geology, College of William and Mary—for inviting me to submit a manuscript to a special issue of an education journal and for encouraging me to be a co-leader of workshops on innovative teaching.

PETER FISKE, then at Lawrence Livermore National Laboratory—for nominating me to the educational committee of a professional society.

JEFFREY NIEMITZ, Department of Geology, Dickinson College, and KENNETH VEROSUB, Department of Geology, University of California–Davis—for co-leading workshops with me on innovative teaching.

DAVID MOGK, then program officer at a federal funding agency—for providing me the opportunity to review proposals for undergraduate education.

MARGARET (EDIE) PARSONS, a former student in my class—for continuing to give me excellent feedback on the course long after the course was over.

JODY NYQUIST, DONALD WULFF, WAYNE JACOBSON, KAREN FREISEM, LANA RAE LENZ, DEBORAH HATCH, MARGY LAWRENCE, and all the staff at the Center for Instructional Development and Research, University of Washington—for collegial guidance and encouragement in my learning about teaching and learning.

ELIZABETH GORDON (HOUSEL), a former student in my class—for co-leading workshops on cooperative learning with me, pushing me to train other faculty in cooperative learning, and continuing to carry the torch for innovative teaching.

SHIRLEY MALCOM, American Association for the Advancement of Science—for suggesting I write a book, and JOHN DELANEY, School of Oceanography, University of Washington—for saying "ditto."

MARY DEANE SORCINELLI, Center for Teaching, University of Massachusetts Amherst—for paving the way for me.

JAMES ANKER, Publisher, Anker Publishing Company—for taking a chance on me.

THOMAS HINCKLEY, College of Forest Resources, University of Washington—for reading and criticizing a rough draft of the manuscript.

CAROLYN DUMORE, Anker Publishing Company—for excellent editorial support.

and spanning this entire chronology

TOMILYNN MCMANUS, my wife—for her support in too many ways to list.

1

BEFORE THE CHANGE

The Post-doc Days

It was a pleasant day in October when I drove in to Seattle; it was a glorious day for me. I had passed my dissertation defense, some 2,000 miles behind me, and zoomed away in my new sports car. Debt was my passenger. I was eager and thankful to have a job awaiting me at the University of Washington (UW). It's true that the job happened not to be in the petroleum industry, in which I had planned to work before the economy slumped. It was in academia. And it did happen not to be in the sub-discipline of geology that was my doctoral research, but in a distantly related sub-discipline of a different discipline, oceanography. And, of course, it was a post-doc position, not a real job. But it would pay me a salary, and the description of the work interested me. The work, as you would expect, was research.

For the next two years I was a member of a large team studying the geology of the sediments on the floor of the Chukchi Sea in the Arctic Ocean, and the biology, chemistry, and physics of the overlying waters. My research was on the sediments—sampling the sea floor on cruises, analyzing samples in the lab, writing technical reports and a paper or two, giving talks at scientific meetings. What I didn't do was teach, advise students, or serve on committees, nor did I want to. Nor was I expected to. I was a typical post-doc at a research university.

As the end of the contract period approached, I was asked whether I wanted to stay in the department. A new research contract was to be awarded, and I could be a member of the new team. I liked doing research; the new project interested me. I liked the people I was working with, and—let's be honest—where else would I go? So, I stayed.

There was a catch to the agreement, however. My mentor "urged" me to learn more oceanography so that I could better fit my research results into the wider context of the natural processes that are active in the ocean. He was persuasive. Granting him the point, I suggested that my sitting in on some oceanography courses would be a splendid (and familiar) way to learn. To which he replied that the best way to learn something was to teach it. He was kidding me. Wasn't he? He wasn't. This did not sound promising.

While a graduate student, I had been a teaching assistant (TA) in a few labs, but I had never been taught how to teach. I just followed through on the lab exercises that had been used before. There had been no reason to think about teaching. Teaching was just something you did, and I hadn't planned to work in academia, anyway. But come my third autumn at the UW, I would teach the evening introductory course in oceanography: 7 p.m.–9:10 p.m., Tuesdays and Thursdays, and thereby begin, although I was not aware of it, what would turn out to be my teaching career.

In answer to my question about how to prepare for the course, I was told to borrow the lecture notes from a faculty member who was known to teach it very well. And so I did. (No wonder teaching hasn't changed much. The lecture notes are passed on.) I still have my lecture notes for that course, probably because they are the only lecture notes that I ever kept in a three-ring binder. (I was not about to let a page fly off the lectern and leave me with nothing to say.) Some pages are indeed my rewriting of the other fellow's notes, but most are straight copies of his notes.

I can't tell you what was on my mind as I began to teach the 41 students in that course, for I kept no diary or journal, only a few notes to myself. Being young, I was probably anxious over not grasping the content well enough to teach it, because practically all the content I would be teaching was new to me, and apprehensive that I would not present it well. I had received more instruction on working aboard the research vessel—don't step in the bight of a line, go to the lee rail to throw up—than on teaching in the classroom. But let's face it, lecturing was merely something you did. It was sort of "everybody does it, anybody can do it." I'm certain that I didn't think about lecturing technique. Nor would there have been reason to think about the purpose of the course. After all, it was a survey course. I had taken survey courses as a student; I knew what they were. They briefly treated principal topics in the discipline, and the students were there to learn about those topics.

And so I stumbled into the habit of teaching. If we take Covey's (1990) definition of habit as "the intersection of *knowledge, skill,* and *desire*" (p. 47), then I had assumed the knowledge of what to do and why to do it—teach the students about the topics; I had defined the skill of how to do it—lecture; and I had faked the desire to do it by designating it a duty. I have a feeling that at a research university duty is too often the third component of this habit. One basis for this assumption is the faculty's use of research money to buy out, and thus reduce, their teaching time.

A classic story of replacing teaching time with research time is that of the physicist Percy Bridgman of Harvard University some years ago. He was so dedicated to his pioneering, Nobel research on high-pressure physics that he did not teach undergraduate courses, did no administration, had few graduate students, served on few committees, and once told the president of Harvard, "I am not interested in your college, I want to do research" (Kemble & Birch, 1970, p. 35). He is said to have got away with his audacity because he had heard that you could if you were good enough in what you did. But for me, it was teaching time.

I listed the 14 topics from the other fellow's notes in my outline of the course, the old, reliable "Table of Contents" version of a course outline, a favorite of generations of instructors. Here is what I wrote on the first page of my lecture notes: "[The course] is a brief survey of important physical, chemical, biological, and geological aspects of the ocean and an introduction to scientific study." In retrospect, this statement of purpose is typical and accurate for an introductory course at a research university—and utterly jejune.

In the second year that I taught the course, I better structured the outline. For each class period of the term, the following information was listed: the topics to be lectured on, the reading assignment in the textbook, and other assignments. I am obviously a highly organized, highly structured person—even though I owned a sports car. The outlines of my courses in later years never varied much from this template. Nevertheless, this preference for structure would not prevent me from finally changing my teaching to a method that appears chaotic to some observers. So don't assume that a preference for structure will impede your changing the way you teach.

There is another point of interest about this outline. It has to do with the seclusion of the instructor on the classroom island and the respect accorded that seclusion by the rest of the faculty at a research university. There was no need for me to tell the faculty what I did in the classroom; there was no need for them to ask me. One thing I did was to eliminate the final topic of the course: life in the sea. Why? Let's say that I concluded there was too much material to cover. I simply lopped off the tail of the course, so to speak, even though, as some student evaluations remarked at the end of the course, it was the opportunity to learn more about life in the sea that had attracted most students to the course. But how was I supposed to know that? Surely I wasn't expected to ask them why they were taking the course. No professor had ever asked me that question. (My decision was also guided, I'm sure, by my not knowing very much biology.) And, yes, the feeling that I was an imposter, posing as an oceanographer, gnawed at me as I unwittingly succumbed to the "imposter syndrome" in teaching (Brookfield, 1995, The Imposter Syndrome [Reminder: Information following the year of publication in a parenthetical citation refers to a heading or subheading in the work cited]). With relief I scurried back to my research.

The next year I substituted two lectures on a topic of interest to me for two lectures on a topic that I had found very difficult to teach—in fact, very difficult to understand. Then I learned that the deleted topic was of great interest to people who lived around Puget Sound, my new home. This realization shook me, because it convinced me that I was indeed an imposter, pretending to be an authority on the ocean. Although changing topics was one way for me to deal with my anxiety, it was obviously not the best way. But in the splendid seclusion of the classroom it was an easy way out. I also knew that as long as I was lecturing, no one could ask me a question to expose my ignorance, which seemed to me barely concealed. Today I believe that part of that anxiety must have been fueled by my imagination, for on rereading the students' comments about the course, I find the students remarked that I took time to answer "special questions" (but it's beyond me, though, to tell you what made those questions "special").

Although I was in over my head at times in teaching oceanography, my research over the next few years was succeeding, even prospering:

principal investigator or co-principal investigator on several research grants, published papers, oral presentations at scientific meetings. Those research accomplishments and an acceptable teaching record earned me the title of assistant professor and with it a move from the research faculty to the teaching faculty. (Without a doubt, the research accomplishments were the basis for the promotion. I could have as well been promoted with no teaching experience, an experience gap common to most new assistant professors, even today.)

Team Teaching

I then began taking on more teaching responsibilities, most of which were, thank goodness, as a member of a team of instructors. Not having responsibility for the whole course relieved my anxiety. Oceanography, being a truly interdisciplinary subject, is tractable to team teaching, and so I found myself a member of two teams. One team taught the large day course in introductory oceanography. The other taught the senior-level course that later would be the course in which I left the lectern. It was mainly in this team-teaching environment that my teaching ability developed for many years. In an attempt to recall for this book how on Earth I did develop as a teacher, I have read some records of my early teaching, which, because either I am part pack rat or I forget to throw things away, I happened to keep. These records form the basis for this story of my development.

Brookfield (1995) discusses four kinds of records from which we can learn about our teaching: 1) our self-reflection, 2) student comments, 3) peer review, and 4) our reading in the education literature. Let's take each of these in turn, beginning with self-reflection, which is quickly disposed of because I didn't do it, not with any depth. Why would I? What would I have thought there was to reflect on? All that was expected of me in teaching was to get the content right and get it to the students in a reasonably coherent form. I tried very hard to do that. Content that I had trouble getting right, I simply replaced with other content, a faculty trick that I have found to be not uncommon. It was understood that lecturing was just talking. You trained to give good research talks at scientific meetings by practicing giving talks at brown-bag lunches. You learned to talk by talking. So you learned to teach by teaching, same difference. It was not as though we were teachers in elementary or secondary schools, where you deal with children or adolescents; we were teaching university students. So we obviously needed no preparation to teach. It was like learning to ride a bicycle. Just do it. I never reflected on my ability to ride a bicycle.

Now and then I did write on my lecture notes some reminders to myself about changes to make the next time I taught that part of the course, such as changing the order of topics or using a different example. Tucked into these little reminders were clues to reorganizing the way I taught, as discussed in Chapter 3. But these were minor adaptations of content. Nothing set me to wondering why I was there or how I could improve what I was doing. I was confident that I was teaching what and how I was supposed to be teaching. After all, as far as I knew, I was doing what other faculty were doing, had always done, and had done to me when I was a student. I was doing what I ought to do. So why would I have thought that I should reflect on my teaching?

The second kind of record for learning about our teaching is student comments. As you know, they can be obtained in various forms, not that I wanted to receive them in any form in those days. The most lasting of these records are the anonymous comments that students write on the course evaluations at the end of the term. I dreaded the day they arrived. I would read them quickly, skimming over the favorable comments, to suffer in anguish and indignation from the wallops of such complaints as my not showing enough interest in the material, not being dynamic, and being boring. Did they really think that I was supposed to entertain them? They had to take me as I was. Other complaints, like excessive length of the reading assignments, were taken by all members of the team as typical student complaints about too much work. We were the experts. We knew what readings were important and significant for them to know. The students should try harder. Nevertheless, the pain of the complaints was always greater than the solace of the compliments. Then I would file the evaluations away and forget them. Rarely did they cause me to change a part of my teaching.

I had lots of excuses for not changing my teaching to meet the complaints in those comments. For instance, the comments were written at the end of the course, a time when I was not interested in thinking about the course any more for a year. Besides, those students would never be in that course again, anyway. If the course was the large introductory course, I might not even see those students again. There was always the possibility—or my yearning—that the students who took the course the next year would be more receptive and appreciative of the information that I supplied them. In the senior-level course there were both undergraduate and graduate students. Perhaps it was the graduate students who wrote that the course dragged, while the undergraduate students appreciated the slow pace. But I didn't create the student composition of the course. That was their problem. Why should I worry about what I couldn't change? Nor did the student evaluations come with an offer from the department or the university to help me improve my teaching. In sum, the students' comments were not much help in developing my teaching ability.

The third kind of record that can inform us about our teaching is peer review. I'm sure that no member of the team had ever heard of the peer review of teaching. In courses taught by a single instructor, no other faculty member would have dared to violate the instructor's seclusion and "review" his or her teaching, whatever that might mean beyond whether the content was accurate and presented well. In the team-taught course, each instructor would have had to be reviewed. (A better term for the structure of this course is one I heard used by a colleague from Stanford University: "tag-team teaching." Although the coordinator of our course attended every class period, each instructor would attend only to teach his own section of the syllabus and then "tag" the next team member to take his place in the ring and throw the students to the mat with more information, and so on throughout the course.)

What would we discuss about teaching with a peer reviewer? So I could be boring! Who was going to tell me how not to be boring? Certainly no one I knew. So what if the students thought another instructor seemed not to care whether they learned the information! Every member of the team would have said that learning was the students' responsibility, not ours. What could any of us have done about it? As I said, we never considered peer review of our teaching.

The fourth and final kind of record is the record of our reading in the education literature. Well, I didn't even know there was an education literature. And if I had known, I wouldn't have thought I had a reason to read about teaching. If the teaching wasn't broken, why read about fixing it? And there you have the four kinds of records from which we can learn about our teaching. None of us was aware of three of them, and we ignored the other one.

I wasn't smug about my teaching during this time, mind you. I was always anxious about the loose fit of that "mantle of authority." There I was, standing at the lectern in front of the class to give them the correct information. But what if I screwed up, said something incorrect, was caught not knowing the answer? What—dare I say it?—if the students were to correct me? For several years, I wore a white lab coat to class, not because I had just come from the lab, but because it concealed the damp tension blotches that waxed darkly on my shirt as I lectured. Teaching was not a joy. It was a duty. (Years later I read and enjoyed Parker Palmer's inspiring book, *The Courage To Teach* [1998]. But when he adverted to "the passions that took us into teaching" [p. 21], I'm afraid a big snort of derision escaped me.)

Now, please don't take what I have just written to mean that I didn't care about my students, for I did. I believe it the rare professor who doesn't care about them and want them to learn the information presented. I am just describing the educational environment in which I taught—and taught with absolutely no reason to question its validity. I thought my students were learning. After all, I—a professor—had learned that way. The students did pretty well on my exams, which they kept telling me were impossible for them to study for, as though it was my responsibility to tell them what to study for. The questions on the exams usually required more of them than repeating what I had told them. Some questions were problems; I thought them probing; the students thought them "picky." But the fairly good grades on the exams told me the students must have learned the material.

I have to say, though, that I really didn't know the students. I usually entered the classroom, unnoticed by my students, and went to the front, opened my notes on the lectern, tested the overhead projector, arranged my overhead transparencies, and then, head down, silently studied—or pretended to study—my notes until the bell rang and I had to begin the lecture. Now and then a student would come to me with a question before class started. Meanwhile, the classroom was abuzz with laughter and chatting. During the lecture, the students seldom asked questions; they scribbled away in silence. What more could I have asked of them? Silent, attentive students—passing over the occasional dozer! It was the perfect classroom. Then, lecture over, the students would chatter loudly amidst the bumps and clatter of collecting their belongings and they would leave, while I would silently gather my notes and overheads and trail after them, unremarked. Everyone behaved naturally.

I knew only a few of the students by name. I saw no reason to take roll. After all, the students were adults. For years the TA graded the exam papers. I rarely saw the students' names. My relationship with the students was impersonal, not that I disliked them by any means. No doubt they were fine young men and women. It was just the way things were. It was my job to teach; it was their job to learn. If they had any difficulty in learning, I expected them to come to me for help. That few of them did told me pretty clearly that they were not having difficulties. When a student did come for help, I eagerly told him or her the answer, for I was very glad to help. (By the way, that so many of them could be absent on any given day and still pass the exams showed me they knew how to study.)

A Disaster

Let's move ahead a few years in the senior-level course that I eventually changed. We were still a team of four instructors, each teaching the same part of the course every year. As the years passed, my student evaluations recorded an improvement in my teaching, and I paid a little more attention to them. They said that I was open to questions, even—to my amazement today, since I don't remember this—in some years soliciting and answering questions at the beginning of each class period. The students wrote that I emphasized significant points and tried to make sure they understood the information. But, yes, I was still boring, my exams were confusing, and my reading list was too long. As I have said, there was nothing I could do to moderate those complaints: I was me, exams were exams, the reading list was mine. What was there to change?

Then, my teaching in the course fell apart. Perhaps I had gone stale from teaching the same information for so long. Perhaps I had accepted too many demands on my time: adjunct appointments in another department and a research institute; committee meetings in the departments, in the university, and nationally; release time to help draft a national report; and several other opportunities of the kind that come our way as professors. I couldn't bring myself ever to say no. Whatever the cause, my teaching in the course aroused student complaints too serious to ignore: pick up the pace, cover more material, condense the lectures, drop the attempts at time-consuming class participation, show some enthusiasm. Although some students appreciated my good organization, willingness to take questions, and attempts to involve the class in discussion, I clearly wasn't being effective, and I naively thought that discussions were self-propagating, like bull sessions. I could no longer ignore the students' complaints. I had to react. I needed help with my teaching, but, as far as I knew, that help could come only from me.

The only improvement I could think to make was to change the content I taught. After all, teaching was all about content. And so I introduced into my lectures the historical development of the concepts. In hindsight, I see that I was thinking of my interest in history, not the students' needs. Well, I bombed—but good. (I had no grasp of the effective role of historical perspective in the teaching of science [American Association for the Advancement of Science Project 2061, 1990]). The evaluations were devastating, summed up in too much history, too little science. Once again, I set out to change the content in reaction to the students' complaints. It never occurred to me that I lacked a guiding principle. I dumped the history, and the following year recast the information in the fashion of a hot new concept, with some success. I assumed I was in recovery, only to be shocked the very next year by the departure of the other three members of the team, five weeks before the term began. Was that how it felt to sink whimpering into quicksand?

It would have been useless for me to borrow their lecture notes to teach the other three parts of the course. The situation was not the same as when I had borrowed notes to teach my first evening course. Each of the four parts of this course was highly specialized, and we had never coordinated the content, even though some of the students had asked us to do so. Each part stood firmly by itself. I was sinking deeper into the quicksand. With less than five weeks of crash preparation—while knowing full well it was hopeless—I taught the course to the bitter end, an utter disaster. I'm embarrassed to say I was reduced to reading some material to the class directly from the textbook. That term I marked an "X" through the date on the wall calendar in the morning when I arrived at the office, rather than in the evening when I left.

That was spring term. Fall term would come with a new curriculum, which would place the graduate students and the undergraduate students in separate courses and pair me with another professor as a team of two. Hallelujah! He brought a different perspective to a part of the course I couldn't teach, and I tried to pull the rest of the course together as best I could with the luxury of more time to prepare. The result, according to the student evaluations at the end of fall quarter, was a slight improvement in my teaching. Even a slight improvement was cause for champagne. Soon the undergraduate course became mine to teach alone.

My Own Course

As I look through my lecture notes for the course over the years leading up to this point, I find only two comments about teaching that though mainly about content are not solely about content. The first was written early in my team-teaching experience. On the first page of my notes I wrote what I expected the students to learn: "What to get out of this section—1) distribution of deep-sea sediments on the ocean floor, 2) general description." Talk about vague expectations! And don't they hint of looming memorization? The second comment about teaching was written a few years later when I was coordinating the course. It is a more thoughtful statement about learning, for it is a list of the recommendations for improving the course that were offered by the students in an open discussion on the last day of the term. The recommendations included better relating to this course what the students were learning in the other oceanography courses, passing out the handouts prior to lecturing, and making our expectations for the students clearer. The plea for clearer expectations would go unanswered for most of my teaching career because, without pondering the matter, I expected them to know everything I taught them.

Let me repeat that, for absurdity often slips by us undetected: I did not set forth clear expectations. I now believe that I made no explicit expectations because that would have required me to establish priorities. If, however, students are expected to learn everything they are taught—because if it were not important, why in the ever-loving world would I have taught it to them in the first place?—then there are no priorities to set; that is, no decisions for me to make. And so we have a notion about student learning that on the surface appears rigorous, but at the core is absurd and self-serving for the teacher. How many times over my years of teaching had the students made pedagogically sound recommendations that we instructors ignored! These three recommendations were likely ignored as well, probably having been judged as evidence that the students wanted to be led rather than to think for themselves. To lead them was not our responsibility. We couldn't learn it for them.

These were the conditions in which I developed as a teacher. I accepted them fully. In fact, I would not have sought to change them. So it's easy for me to understand why someone now teaching like that would find it difficult to contemplate changing. Except for a few pitiable years, the conditions were not too bad—for me. They molded me into an organized but boring lecturer who gave confusing exams and overlong lists of assigned reading, but who cared about whether his students learned the information even though that care was expressed so ineptly that he could not state clearly what he expected of the students.

The students must have learned something. After all, it was the system in which I had learned, as had most of the faculty, I'm sure. That the system had weaknesses—especially for students who were not planning to become future faculty like me, students who did not thrive on academic learning—never entered my mind. To take one example of weakness, let's look at a basic principle of good practice in undergraduate education today, one that sets the stage for enhancing student learning by paying attention to "the knowledge and beliefs that learners bring to a learning task" (Bransford, Brown, & Cocking, 1999, p. 11). The principle is to encourage contact between students and faculty (Chickering & Gamson, 1987), but it can be stated in plain English as "Know your students."

Although there are methods to apply this principle (Davis, 1993, The First Day of Class; McKeachie, 2002, Meeting a Class for the First Time), the principle was not applied in the conditions in which I taught. I have told you that I really didn't know my students—they were oceanography majors, period—and that I would never have considered asking students why they were taking a course of mine and what they knew and believed that was relevant to the course. To do so would have been both unnecessary—for I had already written my lecture notes—and unseemly. And I was totally unconscious of the effect that my way of teaching might have on the learning of a student from a different race or ethnic background from mine (Davis, 1993, Diversity and Complexity in the Classroom: Consideration of Race, Ethnicity, and Gender).

But think for a moment: When a piece of technology that you use goes on the blink and you seek assistance in a technical manual that was written by someone who, though well grounded in the content of technology, obviously doesn't "know his audience," how satisfied are you with the content presented? Yeah, you don't use the manual again. If you go to the performance of an entertainer who, though proficient in her art, obviously doesn't "know her audience," how satisfied are you with the wrong kind of entertainment for the audience? If you shop at a business that, though offering the service or product you want, doesn't "know its customers," how satisfied are you with the unsatisfactory service or product? Similarly, if we don't "know our students," we risk not satisfying their search for knowledge (learning) as fully as we can.

How many performances can that performer give without knowing her audience before there is no audience? How many customers can that business displease before there are no customers? But the writer of the technical report and the professor in class have nothing to worry about. The technology user can bypass the manual and try to find answers online or at a call center. The writer becomes irrelevant. And professors are monopolists. Students have no alternative sources for the knowledge they seek. None of this did I know then. Reflecting on my ignorance, I'm reminded of my junior-high-school English teacher who, on occasions of my display of ignorance, would alter Thomas Gray's lines "Where ignorance is bliss / 'Tis folly to be wise" to "Where ignorance is bliss / Dean is the biggest blister around." I was a big blister of ignorance about the need to know my students.

Although I had made some small incremental changes in content over the years, some of which had helped, but one of which had sunk me, I had not faced change in any other form. Now I began to make small changes in other ways, in what I did and in what the students did. Without thinking of it, I was beginning to change behaviors. I didn't know why or what I wanted for the class or how to get it, but I knew something had to change. With each change there lay in wait a risk. At bottom lay the risk of failure.

Reflective Questions

- *What was the first course you taught?*

- *How much preparation did you receive for teaching that course?*

- *Would you have undertaken your first research with the same amount of preparation as you had for your teaching?*

- *If not, why not?*

- *What does that answer tell you about your attitude toward teaching?*

- *Why are you reading this book?*

- *Which characteristics of teaching mentioned in this chapter also apply to your teaching?*

- *Which do not?*

- *How would you describe the difference between the two lists?*

2

CHANGE INVOLVES TAKING RISKS

Anxiety Upon Anxiety

Before discussing how I changed the way I teach so that students were taking a more active part in their learning, I must discuss an aspect of teaching that I have so far only mentioned. It is an aspect we shun in an attempt to deny its existence. Yet exist it does. It is the fear of teaching. Yes, the fear of teaching, a notion we either scoff at in surprise or recognize in silent shame. Which of those reactions was evoked in you on my mentioning this indignity? When I first read about it—long after the time we are at in my story—I scoffed, and why not? What is there to fear in teaching? Before I answer that question, let's be more precise in our use of terms.

Although the fear of teaching is indeed a subject for discussion (e.g., Palmer, 1998, A Culture of Fear), the use of the word "fear" can be easily perceived on first reading as an exaggeration and the notion dismissed as fantasy, for fear is commonly aroused by a danger external to us and it often implies a loss of courage. The fear of teaching, however, does not necessarily entail a loss of courage in the classroom and only very rarely an external danger—yet. (As the first outbursts of deadly violence worked their way up through secondary schools, we complacently assumed they would never reach higher education, but they have. Even worse violence is following. A disturbed student bursting into our classroom, gun in hand, would indeed evoke fear, but that condition is not our topic.)

Jersild (1955) makes the case that anxiety rather than fear, is our concern. He describes anxiety as

> a state of distress, uneasiness, disorder, or disturbance
> arising from some kind of stress within the personality.
> The essential feature of this stress is that it is due, at

least in part, to inner or subjective conditions as distinguished from external or objective threats and dangers.
(p. 27)

Anxiety disrupts us from within. Therefore, he proposes that

the concept of anxiety should be regarded as a key concept in education. . . . Anxiety is an important element
in the personal lives of teachers, and it penetrates variously into the lives of all pupils. If in education we try
to evade anxiety, we thereby try to evade the challenge
of facing ourselves; we evade an essential task and make
added trouble for ourselves and others. (p. 26)

My reason for making this distinction between fear and anxiety,
which I admit can blur on occasion, is that whereas we might scoff at the
notion of being afraid in the classroom, we might at least consider the
possibility that on some occasions in the classroom we are anxious. Think
about it: anxiety—that distress of mind that arises on anticipating
impending failure. Think about the distress that can be produced in us if
there is a difference between what we are (a well-trained and acclaimed
researcher) and what we pretend to be (an effective classroom teacher)
and then if something the students do seems to threaten that pretense.

Here are a few situations that can provoke anxiety in teachers, labeled
"fear" by some authors, and a reason why, as taken from Jersild (1955),
Kraft (2002), and Palmer (1998), with a few situations of my own. Feel
free to add to the list from your experience:

- A conversation with a student over a grade. It may become
  win/lose (competition) and we don't want to lose to a student.

- A student in lecture whose posture and manner dares us to teach
  him or her. We are drawn to the challenge, ignoring the other
  students; yet we may not succeed.

- Students do not react to our subject matter with enthusiasm.
  It threatens the intellectual validity of our subject matter.

- A group of students begins to carry on a conversation. It may not be to clarify or expound on a point just made.

- A student in discussion or in answering a question says what we don't want to hear. It forces us to face unpleasantness in front of the students.

- A student grimaces during our lecture. It might be a show of disrespect.

- A student suddenly gets up and leaves. She may have been too bored to take any more of the lecture.

- Students don't even try to answer a question we ask them. It suggests they don't value what we are doing.

- Some students in class do not catch on quickly to the content. They remind us that we do not know how to teach students who most need to be taught.

- A student asks a question to which we do not know the answer. It reminds us that we don't know enough to be the experts we profess to be.

- Students exhibit some characteristics that bother us as we age. They are the same characteristics that in our teenage children make us anxious.

Our anxiety can express itself in several forms: an uneasiness with no obvious cause, uneasy anticipation, irritation, annoyance, exasperation, loss of temper, melancholy, lack of fulfillment, and emptiness, to name a few (Jersild, 1955). It is easy for us to blame the students for most of the situations that can cause us anxiety: They aren't motivated, aren't prepared, don't pay attention, and so forth. Certainly they bear a share of the blame, but not all. Or we may deny that we are ever anxious. Denial is easy because we may not know we are anxious (Jersild, 1955) or afraid (Palmer, 1998), or if we do know it we cannot bring ourselves to deal with it. I denied it to myself until I asked myself why I was wearing that white lab coat. I was sweating under that coat, not because I was felling trees or building a house, but because I was anxious as hell. Then there was my feeling of being an imposter. That feeling was surely an anxiety that I might be caught red-handed by the students as not being the expert they expected me to be. And what about you? What anxious situations have you experienced?

So why all this self-flagellation? Because I want you to examine your teaching critically as you follow the story of how I changed mine. If you are like me, you received no instruction in how to teach. Like me, you were thrown into a classroom and told to teach. You coped with it as best you could. Teaching has become a habit. You know the subject matter well enough to teach it. You have developed some skill at lecturing. But rather than possessing the desire to teach, which should be the third characteristic composing a habit (Covey, 1990), you may have settled for just doing what you ought to do. But it is a habit. Although we find comfort in our habits, your habit of teaching can make you anxious. So don't look back on this way of teaching, or "Old Cheese," to use Johnson's (1998) term, as preferable just because it is familiar. Recall that at times it does not satisfy you, and remember, as Covey says, "It's only the unsatisfied need that motivates" (p. 241) one to change.

Examining your teaching with a clear eye is important because I'm proposing that you consider changing the way you teach, which will place another kind of anxiety on top of the anxiety of teaching. It is the anxiety of change, or fear of change (Covey, 1990; Johnson, 1998). It is creating a new habit. Making a change "has to be motivated by a higher purpose, by the willingness to subordinate what you think you want now for what you want later" (Covey, 1990, pp. 47–48). This may sound like I'm asking too much of you. But I can tell you that when I had changed the way I taught, the anxiety of change was over and the anxiety of teaching was greatly reduced.

It's funny that the thought of changing what we do in the classroom can scare us spiritless. We know how to transfer information to students sitting quietly, and we don't want to risk changing that because our comfort with the known is greater than our anxiety of teaching. All our careers, whatever attention we have given to our courses has been to our teaching, our lecturing, not to our students' learning. Many of us don't want to take a doubtful chance, a risk, at emphasizing student learning over faculty teaching; we lose our spirit, for we are afraid we may fail.

And that would make us look foolish in front of our students, the very people to whom we have always tried to present ourselves as the authority, the proverbial fount of wisdom. But this is not the only reason we may be anxious about changing the way we teach.

Some of us worry about attempting to change because we are bored or discouraged with our teaching and lack the enthusiasm to change. A common cause of boredom or discouragement is deadening repetition: We have lectured about the information for so many times that, even though we revise our lecture notes, we still hear ourselves saying the same old thing. It's boring, and boredom is contagious. The students readily catch it from us and, like a bad cold, return it. You'll be surprised at the excitement sparked in you by the students as they learn in a manner that engages their interest in what, for you, is old material.

Finally, let's not forget that there are faculty who feel there is no need to change, because they believe they are already achieving the new goals. My teaching, as described in Chapter 1, is an example from nearly this point of view, for I certainly thought that my students were learning what I taught. The risk of change here is for us to be proven wrong, to be proven naive about teaching.

Regardless of the cause of our doubt about change, for us to try and to fail in front of our students would undermine our credibility and stature, or so it can seem. In addition, there is the risk that our colleagues will disapprove of this change. Even the students may resist the change. All things considered, it's no wonder we can be anxious about attempting to change, even fearful of it. It's a natural reaction.

We Have Done It Before

What is so ironic about this risk avoidance is that we are trained risk takers. And well trained, at that! That's how we got our Ph.D. degrees. We undertook a more or less risky piece of scholarly research, completed it successfully, and received the degree in return. Had there been no risk to the research problem, no possibility of foolish mistake or failure, the problem would not have been approved for our doctorate research in the first place. What's more, all our research since then has contained an element of risk. No one works on trivial problems at a research university and advances academically. We live by taking risks. That's what we're paid to do. But we have carefully consigned that risk to our research and barred it from our classrooms.

Once upon a time we did take risks in the classroom—most recently when we taught our first class. We succeeded, but we locked the door and took precious few risks after that. We took many risks in the classroom when we were students, however. And the threats that awaited us in taking those risks kindled anxiety within us. In fact, anxiety, or fear, is the companion of most students in our classes (Brookfield, 1995; Jersild, 1955; Palmer, 1998). As Brookfield puts it, "One of the hardest things for teachers to do is to imagine the fear that students feel as they try to learn what we teach" (p. 50).

Have you forgotten your own student days, at least in some courses? Remember finding out that the notes you had taken in class were incomplete? That was the risk of taking poor notes. Remember the risk of not understanding the lecture and being afraid to ask a question because you thought you were the only student who didn't understand? Remember the risk of choosing the wrong subjects to study for the exam because you were expected to "know everything" but couldn't possibly memorize it all? In short, remember the risk of getting a low grade in the course? Of course, those were not the courses in our majors. We did well in courses in our majors, otherwise we wouldn't be professors in those disciplines today. But there were other courses that we didn't do so well in. Nevertheless, we passed them. In spite of our anxiety, we took the risk of learning and succeeded. What you did then, you can do now. And you need not just "suck it up" and wade "manfully" or "womanfully" into the change.

Six Steps

As with the preparation for many changes one makes in life, the preparation for changing the way one teaches can be considered in terms of specific steps. There are six steps that can better prepare you to make the change in your teaching so that students can change from passive to active learners.

- Accept your own status as a novice learner.

- Adjust to learning a workplace skill.

- Find and read comments about your teaching.

- Welcome flexibility and adaptation into your classroom.

- Apply your creative ability to help students learn.

- Keep the end in mind.

The first step is to realize that in learning to change the way you teach you are a novice learner. Accepting your lowly status as a beginner is significant because if you are like me, it has been a heck of a long time since you were a novice learner in your career. You have forgotten how a novice learns. Instead, you have been learning in your discipline as an expert learner. Expecting to learn how to change your teaching with the methods of an expert learner will quickly frustrate you and lead you to abandon the task, for as our students could tell us if we but asked them, their learning as a novice differs from our learning as an expert. Recalling this difference will better prepare you to make the change.

Studies of the differences between learning by novices and experts tell us what to look for (Bransford, Brown, & Cocking, 1999; Klein, 1998). For instance, whereas experts can readily detect significant patterns, novices don't even notice patterns. As a novice you will have to pick your way through what you read or are told, without the benefit of being able to place the parts together into a pedagogical whole from the beginning. Nor will some relationships be obvious to you. And of course you will make mistakes while learning. You are not accustomed to this inefficient way of learning. But don't give up. Yes, novice learning is difficult. Just ask your students. In fact, becoming a novice learner in any subject is one way for faculty to experience the anxiety of the students in our own classes (Brookfield, 1995).

At the beginning, you will receive sets of procedures and probably checklists. When I was undergoing staff training at the beginning of my two years as a faculty associate in the Center for Instructional Development and Research at the University of Washington, I had checklists for some procedures in consultation, and for those procedures for which I had no checklists, I made checklists. I loved my checklists. I guarded my checklists. I never went without my checklists. As a novice, I needed them to guide me from step to step through a procedure because I had not yet gained the experience and knowledge to let me know why I was taking each step. Resign yourself to the situation that the knowledge of what to do next won't well up inside you with the ease to which you are accustomed. That knowledge will come with experience. You'll get the hang of it, just as you'll get the hang of knowing what you are and are not able to do in your classroom with the new concepts and techniques. So accept that you will be taking the awkward training steps of a novice. This acceptance is good preparation and will lighten any frustration. Don't be impatient.

Realize that you won't be able to organize the new knowledge as readily as you are accustomed to, because you lack the depth of knowledge to allow that. But it will come. Later you will construct the big picture that you are used to having as an expert learner. Perhaps most important to your successful change is practice. It does little good to be told what to do or how to do it; to learn it you have to do it yourself.

The second step is adjusting to a change in our workplace practice; that is, adjusting to learning the practice of teaching. When was the last time you learned a totally new practice, a new set of skills? Learning a new practice is very different from expanding your knowledge in your discipline. Learning a practice is more about learning "to be" a practitioner than learning "about" a subject (Brown & Duguid, 2000). Although we tend to think of our workplace in academia as being quite different from the workplace in business, some similarities exist, particularly when it comes to learning a practice. In their book dealing mainly with learning in business, Brown and Duguid cite many studies of learning. They report that "learning a practice . . . involves becoming a member of a 'community of practice' and thereby understanding its work and its talk from the inside" (p. 126).

As you will read later, I was fortunate to have learned how to change my teaching by joining just such a community of practice. Knowing the advantage of making the change while in the company of other faculty should better prepare you for the change. Take advantage of opportunities to be a member of a community. Maintaining that community after you have been to a workshop, short course, or summer institute will provide you with the support you need as you begin to apply what you have learned (Kraft, 2002). And remember, what is being asked of you, to join a community of practice, is not a new experience for you. In graduate school, you learned the practice of research and were accepted into the community of research practice in your discipline. So this is merely a new form of an old and successful experience.

The third step in preparing to change may well lie in reflective comments about your teaching written over the years, some written by you, some by students. For instance, comments you have written about your classes may hold some clues. I didn't write many comments, but you have read in Chapter 1 that even in the early years I was commenting in my lecture notes about changes in content that I could or should make the next time I taught the course. We'll look more closely at some later notes in the next chapter. Comments like these reveal an inchoate desire for improvement that may make the change easier for you to accomplish than you now expect. If, however, you do come across comments and they mainly "bash" the students, saying students don't want to work, don't care, don't come to class prepared, then likely you are not really interested in making the change, for bashing the students "conveniently relieve[s] us of any responsibility for our students' problems—or their resolution" (Palmer, 1998, p. 41).

Other comments that I found very useful are the ones written by students for the student evaluation of the course at the end of the term. Yes, those things! You probably threw most of them away, but some may still be in course folders from years gone by or in that overflowing cardboard box on the floor in the corner of the office. I'm not referring to the part of those evaluations that are the standardized questions or statements to be scored from 1 to 5. It is the students' written comments on those evaluations that can be valuable for what we are discussing—not, as you are aware, that I always thought so. Those comments are the students' feedback to us on our teaching, and in the conventional lecture class they and the standardized questions and statements are usually the only feedback on our teaching. As with any feedback mechanism, some of the comments are useful, some are useless. We can recognize the comments made by the students who didn't want to be in the course in the first place. We ignore them. We also ignore the comments filled with effusive admiration. The trick is to go over the comments, searching both the complimentary and reproachful ones for indications that might give a hint that you were moving toward change, perhaps without even being aware of it. Let's look at an example of what I mean.

Back in 1970, three professors team-taught a course by lecturing. There was a question on the students' evaluation of the course that asked the students to comment on the strength of each professor's teaching and on what the professor might change to improve his or her teaching. The professors have kindly allowed me to use their evaluations, and in Table 2.1 I have listed one comment in each category for each professor. Based on this information, would you expect any of these teachers later to have changed the way he or she taught, to emphasize student learning over faculty teaching?

Table 2.1

Examples of Students' Comments on Three Professors' Teaching Strengths and Changes

Professor	Strength *(Features that enhanced learning)*	Change *(Features that distracted from learning)*
A	An excellent prof—he really knew his material and was well organized but sometimes rushed in presentation.	He was impossible to reason with and didn't seem to care if we understood his stuff or not.
B	He had a good attitude toward students and tried very hard to learn our opinions about how the course should be improved.	Everything he brought up was "too advanced to be talked about at this level."
C	Good instructor because he took the time to explain his material with an ear for whether it was going above anyone's head or not.	His speaking could be more dynamic.

If we look at the strengths, we see that all the professors were ranked high, but their strengths were unfortunately undermined by their weaknesses. Professor A's strength was in knowledge of content and course organization. Professor B's strength and professor C's strength were interaction with the students. Now look at the aspects that the students thought should be changed. Aloofness and a lack of empathy were perceived in Professor A, a condition that fits all too easily into an emphasis on content in lecturing. Professor B seems to have had trouble matching the content to the level of the students' existing knowledge, even though interested in improving the course. Professor C was not a good lecturer, but was clearly attuned to the students' needs. In the ensuing years, Professor A never showed an interest in changing the way he taught. His emphasis on faculty teaching was unchangeable, as I think we would expect from the students' comments. Professor B eventually did apply active learning, but to his graduate courses and, along with those students, greatly enjoyed the learning environment. Professor C changed his teaching entirely to active learning as soon as he was introduced to it.

So, you see, some of the comments the students provide us as feedback on our teaching can contain very perceptive observations of our attitudes and behaviors. (In fact, having known these three professors for more than 30 years, I can assure you that every comment listed here was right on target. I can also assure you, by the way, that students learned from all three professors. The question here is not whether students learned, for they did, but which of the professors became part of the reform of undergraduate education to enhance student learning.) A look back at your evaluations with an uncolored eye may reveal that your interest in whether your students were learning was perceived by them. If so, the change in your teaching will probably be that much easier for you.

The fourth preparatory step lies in your willingness to welcome flexibility and adaptation into your classroom. When you lecture every class period, there is little need to vary anything about the course: all lectures are presented alike; students take notes every class period; exams are given as scheduled; homework assignments are due as scheduled. Now, by contrast, you will learn that there are other ways to teach, each of which is a method to help you achieve your goals for the class. One method may be effective in achieving one goal; another method may be better for achieving a different goal. Since you don't know what the methods are at this time, the notion of such flexibility may disturb you. That is to be expected. Just open your mind to accept the opportunity to vary what happens in your classroom.

Rest assured that the choice facing you is not total student independence on the one hand, or a free-for-all on the other. As you gain knowledge about the options open to you, flexibility will take on a specific context. A sense of whether the students are "discovering" and "participating" will help you to accept alternatives more readily. In addition, your adaptation will be assisted by the more well-defined goals you will set for your students. (We'll return to a discussion of adaptation and flexibility in Chapter 8.)

But now, let's consider those goals, and let's consider them for a single course. As you begin to change the way you teach, change only a single course. Always have that one course in mind. You will have your hands full changing just one course. The other courses can come later. Now, if asked what goals you have for that course, wouldn't you probably answer something like: cover the material and have the students learn the material? My fuzzy sense of goals up to this time in my story could pretty well be summed up by that statement. When you look at that answer, however, it is as vague as the answers some students give us when they haven't thought about a concept very deeply. You can better prepare yourself for the change if you think more deeply about your goals now, about what you want to accomplish in the course. But since you haven't had to think deeply about goals before, what possible goals come to mind? A simple way to begin the thought process is to pay attention to the general goals other instructors have set, and you can do it online.

The Center for Teaching (1999) at the University of Iowa has posted online the Teaching Goals Inventory from the classic book by Angelo and Cross (1993, pp. 20–21). This inventory comprises 51 teaching goals that were developed, tested on faculty in higher education, and refined by Angelo and Cross. Not only will you find many goals listed that you have not considered before, but you will be expected to rate each goal from essential (one that you always or nearly always try to achieve) to not applicable (a goal that you never try to achieve). You can compare your results to the results of a large number of other instructors. And you will be asked to pick the statement that best fits your conception of yourself as a teacher. This exercise will broaden your notion of teaching and, I think, open your mind to the range of possibilities that awaits you as you begin to change the way you teach. In fact, one surprise that probably awaits you is the large number of goals you will select as essential. Can you really achieve all these goals? How would you do it? These are general goals, remember. You will learn to set particular goals later, from reading a handbook or participating in a workshop or working with a consultant from the teaching center.

Your willingness to take up new ways of teaching will become a part of you. Once you have accepted flexibility as a new part of how you teach, you will be alert to other ways of teaching. We borrow from one another, usually without formal acknowledgment, and we adapt what we borrow to fit the needs of our class. As the course progresses, we may even change what we had planned for class tomorrow in order to solve a classroom, teaching, or learning problem that arose today. Adaptation and flexibility! Your freedom in the classroom will expand. Welcome it! Don't be afraid of it.

The fifth preparatory step is your willingness to be creative in helping students learn. The challenge is not to put together interesting lectures, although that is important. The challenge is to create effective ways for your students to learn what you want them to learn. You begin to concentrate on what you want the students to take away from the course, rather than on what you put into the course. Not until you can recognize some of the problems students face in learning and appreciate the manner in which you can address those problems will you begin to accept new teaching tools and to create your own teaching tools. Think about it: For perhaps the very first time you will take the creative ability that you have used for years in your research and apply it to your teaching, or more accurately, to your students' learning. It will be a new experience, and because of that the notion may seem vague at this time.

When 40 recipients of the MacArthur Awards, familiar as the "genius awards," were interviewed (Shekerjian, 1990), they revealed some of the characteristics that underlie their creative abilities. One characteristic was possession of the required talent. Since your talent for teaching has likely never been explored, you do not know the depth of it. It may be deeper than you think. So don't worry about it at this time.

Another characteristic was perseverance. Here is where it will help you to remember that you are beginning as a novice learner, learning a new practice. It will take time, and you will make mistakes and find some aspects of the change outlandish, but stay the course. Joy awaits you, in the same sense as when an experiment in research goes well, however you define "well." Another characteristic was tolerance for ambiguous circumstances. (Is this what makes research so much fun?) And yes, once you are freed from the highly structured lecture environment, you will live amidst ambiguity. Speaking as a highly structured person, I found it not to be so bad as it first seemed. In fact, it was exciting. Another characteristic was the possession of a solid base of knowledge. At present, you lack a knowledge base of pedagogy. You will learn it from workshops, handbooks, the staff at your teaching center, colleagues in your community of practice, and by just doing it; that is, by just applying the methods creatively in your classroom.

The last characteristic was willingness to take risks. Yes, we're back to that, and to the underlying question that was asked of the MacArthur Fellows: Where does the courage come from to take those risks? You will be glad to know that the Fellows did not ascribe it to self-confidence. So if you are feeling humble about this endeavor, take heart. The Fellows relied on "something perceived as distinctly larger than their own tiny vulnerable beings" (Shekerjian, 1990, p. 25). You will assemble that larger "something" as you learn more about teaching. Parker Palmer's (1998) book is not called *The Courage to Teach* for nothing.

The sixth and final preparatory step is to keep the end in mind. Covey (1990) advises us:

> To begin with the end in mind means to start with a
> clear understanding of your destination. It means
> knowing where you're going so that you better under-
> stand where you are now and so that the steps you take
> are always in the right direction. (p. 98)

Johnson (1998) recommends envisioning yourself finding something better. When I began, I didn't know where I was going or have a vision of something better. You probably don't either, at this point. I was learning techniques. I hope that by reading this book and answering the reflective questions at the end of each chapter, you will be better able to state where you are going, envision something better with less anxiety, and visualize what your classroom may be like after you have changed the way you teach. Helping you visualize this end is the principal objective of this book. The six steps in this chapter will better prepare you to make the change. Now let's begin the story of my change.

Reflective Questions

- *Which course are you going to change? Why that one?*

- *What situations have caused you anxiety while teaching that course?*

- *How will you cope with the challenge of being a novice learner?*

- *How can your own experience in learning new research techniques and methods, as well as helping your students learn them, prepare you to learn new teaching skills?*

- *Where have you stored documents that may contain comments about your teaching?*

- *In which of your common activities do you enjoy being flexible and adaptable?*

- *When will you take the Teaching Goals Inventory?*

- *What are three of your creative accomplishments in your daily non-teaching life?*

- *What is the main risk you are taking in changing your teaching? Keep it in mind so that you can discover sources of strength to overcome it.*

- *At this time, what is your initial vision of your class after you have changed the way you teach it?*

3

CHANGE CAN BE PIECEMEAL

Those Reflective Comments

Faculty can be quick to cut and run before even considering how they might begin to change the way they teach. (Don't let that notion nudge you toward the door.) An all too handy excuse given to me for this behavior is that they don't have time to sit down and work out changes for the whole course. Although you certainly can change the whole course, you don't have to. I didn't. You can make the change step by step. This is easier to do when you have the end in mind so that you know where you are going. Nevertheless, you may already have taken some of those preliminary steps without thinking of them as being part of changing the way you teach.

I was surprised to find that my lecture notes for the first course that I taught, notes I had not looked at for years before writing this book, contained a few reflective comments in the margin that indicated I had begun making changes while teaching my first course. As I have mentioned, most of them dealt with reorganizing the topics or adding or dropping topics, but a few dealt with presentation. For example, beside the lecture notes for one topic is a marginal scribble, "very unsatisfactory," in triple underline, no less. The section on another topic is condemned: "This is terrible!!" An abbreviated comment suggests a different presentation for a concept that is particularly difficult for students to understand on first hearing, but the comment is crossed through, apparently a record of the failure of that presentation. No sign of what happened next. Finally, a diagram sketched on the back of a page of notes as an alternative illustration of a certain natural process bears the comment: "This works very well on the blackboard."

As you can see, most of these reflective comments record my dissatisfaction at not being able to present the material clearly to the class. My guess, in hindsight, is that the dissatisfaction arose from insecurity, from lacking the command of the material that would have enabled me to use a depth of understanding to present the content as simply and clearly as possible. But though restricted solely to content, the comments also must have been my early desultory attempts to enhance student learning. Therefore, if you have written such comments as these in your lecture notes, then you, too, may have already begun to make piecemeal changes in the way you teach. If you haven't, now is a good time to begin.

These comments are one type of information to go in a teaching portfolio (Davis, 1993, Teaching Dossier; Seldin, 2004). For now, though, you aren't interested in creating a teaching portfolio, but you should know what it is. A teaching portfolio is your collection of information about your teaching. Think of it as similar to artists' portfolios of their work, or photographers' portfolios of their work. It contains several types of information about your teaching and your students' learning, some that you create, some that come from your colleagues, and some that come from your students. The basic piece of information is your self-reflective statement about your teaching, which includes your teaching goals, perhaps as you have determined your general goals by completing the Teaching Goals Inventory. The portfolio would also include the changes you made in the materials in the course and in the methods you used to teach that material, your reasons for making the changes, and the results of the changes.

So you see, the little reflective comments on your lecture notes about making even minor changes in the content or the presentation are an inchoate self-reflection, albeit not very critical yet. The teaching portfolio is the collection of all this information. We'll come back to the subject of this portfolio collection from time to time. Incidentally, whereas the teaching portfolio is a record of your teaching in all your courses, either for your use to improve your teaching or for your department's use to consider you for tenure or promotion, there is a course portfolio that you may develop for your use to improve your teaching in a single course (Hutchings, 1998; Peer Review of Teaching, 2001).

Making Small Changes

Let's return to the senior-level course that I changed. We'll consider first the small changes I made in it during the first three times I taught it alone. Then we'll look at a bigger change I made that turned out to be a transitional stage to the final change from lecturing to a form of active learning called cooperative learning.

It will suffice for us to consider active learning as all the formats or arrangements which "require students to *apply* what they are learning" (Meyers & Jones, 1993, p. xi). Many of these activities can be carried out by individual students or pairs of students. (For a more thorough description and various examples, see Meyers & Jones or the following online references: Center for Teaching Excellence, n.d.; McKinney, 2004; Paulson & Faust, 2003.) Some activities require groups of students, such as cooperative learning (Johnson, Johnson, & Smith, 1991; Millis & Cottell, 1998; see online Cooperative Learning Center, n.d.). Other group formats include problem-based learning (Duch, Groh, & Allen, 2001; see online University of Delaware Problem-Based Learning, 1999) and case studies, the latter being common in business, law, and medicine (for science see online National Center for Case Study Teaching in Science, n.d.).

My course met four days a week for 50 minutes. (We are on a quarter term.) It was now my course, after years of team teaching. During the last year or two, I had made a few changes, mainly in the presentation. For instance, I had begun showing slides of the geologic shoreline features I was lecturing on so that students could see what I was describing. I guided students' assigned reading by providing them with study questions. And I even tried writing two or three questions on the blackboard at the beginning of each class period to prime their attention for the important points of the lecture. I cannot take credit for these innovations. I copied them from a couple of colleagues. I also noticed that the other instructor in the course, while we team-taught it, used problem sets (homework) effectively, and I stored away that observation. In other words, I had begun to copy some teaching methods that I saw other instructors use or that I heard about their using. You, however, can discover other teaching methods more easily. You can read about them in the books I have cited, in other books, on the web, or from the staff at the teaching center on your campus, as well as from colleagues.

Because the course was no longer team-taught, now I had to cover all the topics, which meant I had to expand my lecture notes, always a lengthy task. The course outline was the usual list of topics, one or more for each day. I also had my own outline, however, on which I noted what I actually covered in each class period. What I covered was invariably less than what I had planned to cover, a situation that would call for adjustments before the end of the term.

Although I see from my notes for the first day of class that I told the 25 students "class time will be more question and discussion than lecturing," I'm sure the long list of topics caused me to lecture all the time. The significant point, however, is not that there was little discussion but that I would have had the gumption to tell the class to expect more question and discussion than lecturing. I obviously wanted to change the way I taught but didn't know how to make the change and fell back into just covering the material, the easy way out, the old habit.

On the first day of class I also asked the students about their main sub-disciplinary interest in their oceanography major, which was my first attempt to learn something about my students. I found out that most of the students in my marine geology course were biological oceanographers, not marine geologists and geophysicists, but I did not make use of the information in the way I taught the class. It never entered my mind to do so—and if it had, I wouldn't have known how to do it (Davis, 1993, Responding to a Diverse Student Body).

I also had come to know myself well enough as a teacher to realize that I was not comfortable preparing study questions about the reading or attention-guiding questions to write on the blackboard. So I dropped both activities. Rather, I chose to spend my time preparing weekly homework problems, which provided the students with something to do, rather than think about. (I'll elaborate on this "doing" in a moment.) The homework was graded by the TA, an arrangement that continued the TA's responsibilities in the course but also kept me at a distance from the students. In retrospect, I think this arrangement supported my ambivalence toward the students; I wanted to know more about them, but from a distance. The need to distance myself from them must have been grounded in my anxiety. I suppose I could have been lumped into what Palmer (1998) calls a "bad teacher," by which he means those teachers who "distance themselves from the subject they are teaching—and in the process, from their students" (p. 11). But I must have been making progress in overcoming my anxiety, for no longer did I need to wear the white lab coat to class.

I also told the students on the first day that the problems in the homework were of the type that would be on the exams. As you recall, the students had always complained that my exams were impossible for them to study for. My exams consisted of questions about data that would be presented with the exam itself, on a map or chart in the room during the exam, or as a sample on a table. It finally dawned on me that the students had never experienced the situation they encountered during an exam; that is, they had never worked any problems like the exam problems. No wonder they couldn't study for the exams. Now, however, they would have solved some problems in the homework that were of the type on the exam. Although I stumbled onto this improvement in testing the students, I remained ignorant of other aspects of testing that could have enhanced my students' learning (Davis, 1993, Testing and Grading; McKeachie, 2002, Assessing, Testing, and Evaluating).

Probably the most significant little change I made was to begin the practice of writing myself more informative comments about the course for the next year. My first comment suggested revisions in the homework, which I made. It also recommended giving more time for certain topics that I had rushed through, rearranging the order of some topics for a more logical connection, and dropping one topic. Dropping the one topic gave me the extra time for the rushed topics. But oh, the topic I dropped! How I hated to drop it, because I understood this topic very well, unlike topics I had dropped in the past because I didn't understand them. It was some research I had done, and I found it very interesting, so interesting that I wanted the students to know about it. (Did you catch that? "To know about" it! How vague!) But the day I was lecturing on it, a student raised his hand and asked: "Why are we learning this?"

I'll never forget that day. My first thought was: "Why is that student talking to me like this?" I can still picture the classroom, a snapshot, as though looking over my own shoulder toward the student. No one moved. And I can still feel the silence, the long, long, long silence. My cheeks burned. My throat shriveled shut. Finally I mumbled something that was supposed to be coherent. Later in my office, after the shock had worn off, I tried to come up with a better answer, but every attempt was pitiable. They were all pitiable because the student was right: There was no reason for them to learn what I had told them.

I had included the topic because it was about my specialty in the discipline, my own research. (So much for being close to the subject you are teaching!) What is so sad about this incident is that I was totally unaware of being on the receiving end of a teaching moment, or as Palmer (1998) would call it, a "critical moment"; that is, a learning opportunity, in this case for me rather than the students. I dropped my interesting but irrelevant topic, but what I failed to learn from this moment was the need to define what I expected students to learn in my course; call it my goals or my expected learning outcomes (Davis, 1993, Deciding What You Want to Accomplish; Fink, 2003, Appendix A: Planning Your Course: A Decision Guide; McKeachie, 2002, Write Objectives, Goals, or Outcomes). As you have read, that failing had dogged me from the beginning and would continue to do so. It was just too easy for me to say that I wanted them to learn everything I told them. After all, everything I told them interested me. When I began teaching not everything I taught interested me, but all of it had now become important to me.

Examining my course folders for the next two times I taught the course, I see that I kept adding to the course with great enthusiasm. Oh, I added more topics to the outline; each topic was important for them "to know about." I added more papers to the reading list; there were so many really important papers they should "know about." I added displays of the kind of data that would be on the exams. In computing their grade I added to the usual two midterm exams, final exam, and weekly homework, a quiz about shoreline features as shown in 35mm slides and a two-page paper of independent research on a shoreline hazard assessment.

In part, what I was adding to the course were additional ways for the students to do something with data or observations. In an undesigned and unfocused manner, I was making them more active in the course. Being ignorant of the research on student learning, I didn't even think about student learning as a goal, strange as that may sound today. Learning was something that just happened, an activity, not a result. Rather, I took the track of preparing them for the practical needs of employment. For employment, it seemed to me, they needed to be able to do things with what they had learned, although I didn't know just what they should be able to do, having never been employed with a bachelor's degree, nor having talked to employers. That said, I still lectured to them four days a week, unaware of the contradiction between my ill-formed goals of their doing things and my method of teaching that had them merely recording my words.

No longer, however, did I tell them on the first day of class that there would be more questions and discussion than lecturing. I had wised up. Instead, I told them: "I'm assuming you could be a practicing oceanographer a year from now, so I'll treat you more like scientists than students. I'll expect you to learn some fundamentals of marine geology, develop your ability to derive your own opinions by accepting or rejecting observations and data and making different interpretations." It certainly sounds good, doesn't it? But my expectations for them were still vague. I'm sure I had no idea how to achieve those goals.

Nevertheless, I must have been doing something right, for after the second time I taught the course I received my best teaching evaluation thus far and, on the students' nomination, was awarded the College of Ocean and Fishery Sciences award for distinguished undergraduate teaching. That was simply unbelievable. What a thrill! Quite possibly owing to the excitement of receiving that award from the students, I added even more to the course, and as you might guess, I ended up over-tasking the students the next year. I hadn't meant to do that. They were not happy. I sank from a marvelous emotional high to a deplorable low. It was obvious that I had to make a major change for the following year, and I did. Little did I know that the change was actually a transitional change into a completely different type of teaching—and student learning.

Making a Bigger Change

Only by reflecting on those times from my present experience can I see a constancy in my teaching trend: from an early desire for students to apply their knowledge by solving practical problems on exams; through unstructured attempts to engage students in discussion of the information; through wanting them to read about the research results that came from applying the information in various ways; through designing homework problems for them to solve; through testing them by using slides of real-world features for them to identify; to preparing displays of data for them to examine. I obviously had an undeclared goal for the students to "do" something with their knowledge, to use it, not just learn—or memorize—it, but I just as obviously had no vision to contain that goal. I lacked a context in which to think critically about the results that I desired for the students. Probably that was why I began thinking of my teaching in terms of preparing them for employment: It would be the ultimate practical application of their knowledge.

I was unaware that at about this same time educators such as Pat Hutchings, then at the American Association for Higher Education, were putting the desire for students to "do" something with their learning into everyday words: "What matters . . . is not just what students know but what they can do with what they know" (Hutchings, 1990, cited in Meyers & Jones, 1993, p. 6). They were referring to learning, however, instead of employment. I still had not made learning my explicit goal for the course.

My first-day notes for the following year began with the statement from the previous year that I would attempt to treat them more as scientists than students. But there were changes. The director (chair) of the school had graciously approved my request to purchase a large amount of supplies: samples, charts, maps, inexpensive microscopes; that is to say, various visual props and activities. I appreciated his confidence in me. Instead of lecturing all four days, I had the students meet in a lab on Thursdays. In the lab there were wide lab benches with very few utility protrusions interrupting the surface. I used them as large tables. The class period wasn't a traditional lab with experiments and lab notebooks. It was a . . . well, I didn't know what to call it. (In my class folder, I listed these days as "special classes." The use of the term "special" held a greater significance for me than I realized at the time, for these classes were the springboard to cooperative learning.) On the lab tables I spread out charts, maps, data, samples, a few hands-on activities with a question or series of questions by each place. (Owing to a budget cut, I had no TA, but the absence of a TA turned out to be a blessing, as I'll show.)

The students were on their own to walk around the room, sit down at an activity, study the questions, examine the materials, arrive at an answer, and then come to me to check the accuracy of their answer. They were not graded on their answers. They were supposed to apply the information from my lectures and the reading for that week to answer the questions, questions of the kind that would be on the exams. I valued the exercise as an opportunity for them to take the knowledge they had gained from the generalities and examples in both my lectures and the reading and apply that knowledge to the understanding of new examples.

You may question the pedagogical basis for my daring to make such a change in my course—indeed, to take such a risk. Well, I had no pedagogical basis. I had a gut feeling; it told me this is what I should do. Perhaps my development as a teacher had taken me nearer to the next stage in that development (Weimer, 2002, Taking a Developmental Approach), which I'll discuss later. Nevertheless, had anyone told me how significant to "learning" was the transfer of knowledge to other contexts (Bransford, Brown, & Cocking, 1999) and how my little exercises were a crude form of "transfer," they would have been answered with a vacant stare.

You may also protest that I was experimenting on my own students, and you would be correct. I was experimenting on them in the sense of attempting to teach them in a different way, one that would better prepare them for employment. If we do nothing but teach in the way we have always taught, which is itself an experiment, life can go out of our teaching. The Cheese that brings us happiness can lose its taste (Johnson, 1998). To help our students learn, we can even undertake classroom research (Cross & Steadman, 1996) on them; to help us as teachers we must experiment, even though, as Palmer (1998) cautions, "experimentation is risky" (p. 16).

I don't remember what I anticipated my experience in the special class would be; in other words, what I would do during the class period. I certainly was not there to lecture. Nor did I dwell on the risk that the students might think the class period a waste of their time. I was too charged up about the whole thing to care a fig for the risk. It was not self-confidence that I could pull it off; it was a deeper feeling—that what I was doing was right. I do remember expecting the class to be fun, but I couldn't have told you why. Perhaps it was because I would not be lecturing. I was excited about providing the students with the new materials for them to study, to use.

I expected them to come into the lab and each of them to stop at an exhibit, doubling up at times, for there were fewer exhibits than students, and then quietly examine the materials and come to me to verify their answers. Well, they came in and promptly fell into natural groups that casually changed from time to time into new groups. (You can see the first step toward cooperative learning.) They moved around the lab, talking and examining the materials. The room was noisy, which to my astonishment delighted me. When they brought me their answer as a group, I would help them if their answer was wrong.

That they fell into groups of their own accord—remember they were seniors—surprised me, but they did it so naturally and enjoyed the learning environment so much that I now realize the condition prepared me for the ease with which I later turned the course into a cooperative learning format. The old bugaboo that bedevils so many faculty—that a group structure somehow conceals the expression of the individual student's ability—never bothered me.

The fundamental surprise for me, though, was how much more I enjoyed these special class periods than the three days a week of lecturing. I, whose life did not welcome surprises, in school or out, actually preferred the open, flowing, lightly structured special class more than the well-organized, closely controlled, well-structured lecture class. Now, you might say, "Of course you enjoyed it more. You weren't doing anything challenging. You were just answering questions you knew the answers to. Lecturing is hard work." I'll admit that my classroom action wasn't as challenging as delivering a lecture, but designing the problems and framing the questions were certainly more challenging than deciding what content to present. The point was, though, that lecturing did not bring me any joy, even when I knew I had done a good job, such as presenting a key example to demonstrate the application of a concept. No, this joy in the classroom was unique for me. I accepted it. I bathed in it. Had I been told at the time, I would have dismissed the explanation as too touchy-feely, but I now believe that this was the first emotional expression of what Palmer calls the "teacher within," about which he tells us that it says things like "this is what fits you . . ." (Palmer, 1998, p. 31). Oh baby, fit me it did!

The challenge of lecturing, for me, was that I did not know how to improve my lecturing skills. To be perfectly honest, I didn't know they could be improved. I thought I was a poor lecturer, for now and ever more. I had listened to poor lecturers whose advanced age seemed to stand, or slump, as proof that improvement was impossible. As I said about my lecturing in my first course, lecturing was considered something that you simply did. You got up and talked. The requirement for a good lecture was to have the content accurate. If you put the students to sleep with your talk, that inconvenience was merely the price they had to pay to get the information from you. I regret to say: This is still the attitude today in far too many departments at research universities. It is particularly regrettable today because so many opportunities are available for a faculty member to improve his or her lecturing: opportunities with the staff at the university's teaching center, tips on the web, workshops, colleagues, and books, such as Davis (1993, Delivering a Lecture), McKeachie (2002, How to Make Lectures More Effective), and Race (2001).

Some of the suggestions in these handbooks for improving a lecture are easy to accept and execute, such as summarizing what you have said from time to time. Most of them, however, go against the notion of just standing up there and delivering accurate information; for instance, get the students' attention; have an opening, a body, and a closing for the lecture; monitor the students' nonverbal communication for lack of understanding; don't lecture for more than the 10 or 15 minutes at a time that you can hold the students' attention; learn how to vary your voice and delivery; and care deeply about the material.

It's no wonder that I did not start to enjoy lecturing until some years later when I began lecturing on teaching and learning. Very simply, I enjoyed it then because everything I lectured about touched in some way on my experience in teaching and I deeply wished my listeners to enjoy the happiness in their teaching that I had experienced in mine. I was personally involved with the information I presented. By contrast, most of the topics I lectured on in my undergraduate oceanography courses did not touch on my research experience. I was summarizing information that, for implicit reasons, I thought the students "ought to know about," but I was not personally involved with the information. Although I found the information very interesting professionally, there was no emotional attachment to the presentation. No wonder I was boring. Rather than have us use this "conclusion-oriented" mode of lecturing, McKeachie (2002, Planning Lectures) enjoins us as follows: "The lecturer's task in university teaching is not to be an abstractor of encyclopedias, but to *teach students to learn and think*" (p. 55).

So, my three days a week of lecturing did not change. It was the special class that held the innovation. Oh, yes, and I did whack the reading list in half. Another change that the special class held for me was the lessening of distance between the students and me. The closer relation was aided by the lack of a TA, since I graded all the exams, the quiz, and the research paper. For the first time, I wrote the students' nicknames on my class list, for I heard them talking to one another and I saw their names on what I graded. They were Nick, not Nicolaus; Jerry, not Jerald; and Debbi, not Deborah, and I was talking to Nick and Jerry and Debbi. I enjoyed talking to them. I enjoyed the new closeness that displaced the old distance.

Strange as it may seem, only then did it dawn on me that most of the students in my class were women, and a glance through old class lists revealed that women had formed a majority of the oceanography majors for years. The statistics further informed me that for years most of the best students had been women, a fact that had been irrelevant to my teaching. That very irrelevance suggested that my teaching must not have been biased against women, an inference that I deeply appreciated. Whether I had inadvertently not served ethnic and racial minorities so well as I could have, I don't know, for, I'm sorry to say, extremely few minorities major in my discipline—or in any science, for that matter.

It was not until years later, when I read Mitch Albom's (1997) touching book *Tuesdays with Morrie*, that I recognized another blind spot that had afflicted me since the day I taught my first class. In the book Mitch recalls his first day as a student in his first class with Morrie. When his name, Mitchell, was called for attendance as listed on the class list, he was asked whether he preferred "Mitch" or "Mitchell." He had never been asked that question by a teacher. This simple expression of caring not only kept him in the class but set him on the road to become one of Morrie's majors. I read that short sentence and sat stunned, my mind sadly repeating: "I never asked my students that question, never—and I don't know why." Did I not care that much about them? Surely not! Was I as timid with them as all that? I don't know.

I notice from the class folders that for the last time I taught the course before I changed it and eliminated lectures and exams, I stopped introducing it on the first day by saying I was going to treat them more as scientists than students. Instead, I said this: "This is a survey of marine geology. I'm your guide. I'll introduce you to the kinds of problems being studied, techniques being used, and commonly accepted ideas and concepts." On reading this note for this book, I had to smile at the word "guide." I wrote that long before I heard the phrase: replacing the "sage on the stage" by the "guide on the side." My instinct was good, but I was still lecturing, as best I could, for three days a week, while I grew ever more comfortable in the special class.

The students were more comfortable, too. Their evaluations included comments such as: "Lab was great." "You were very interested in whether students were learning the material." "Available and approachable." "You raised questions and provoked original thought." "Information was current and practical." "Labs let us apply lecture knowledge." "Labs let us put lecture concepts to use." "You made us think about concepts not just facts." "We had a lot of free thinking." Comments such as those thrilled me deeply, but they also wrote: "More information on what is expected of us." "You need to state what is expected of us." That unremitting drumbeat—what do you expect of us?—I didn't know how to still it. I stood helpless before them.

Reflective Questions

- *What do you say about your goals or expectations on the first day of class in the course you had in mind when you took the Teaching Goals Inventory?*

- *If you have not told the students about your goals or expectations before, what would you tell them now?*

- *What comments about teaching did you write on the oldest first-day notes that you can find for the course?*

- *How do you interpret any difference between your old comments about teaching and your comments today?*

- *Going back in memory as far as you can, or as far as you have records, write down all the changes you have made in the course. Why is there a trend or lack of trend in this sequence?*

- *How would you like to change the course, whether you know how to change it now or not?*

4

CHANGE IS FINDING AND SHARING ANSWERS TO QUESTIONS ABOUT STUDENT LEARNING

A Critical Question

When, in the midst of our research, we are struck by a question such as "Why did that happen?" or "What did the technician mean by that?" we seek an answer. It is important for us to find an answer because it might affect the outcome of our research. We advance our research by answering questions. But let the very same question arise in the classroom with respect to a student's performance—"Why did that happen?" or "What did the student mean by that?"—and, well, we dismiss it with a shrug and continue what we were doing. We may dub the student a loser and feel no responsibility to probe the situation. We may place no value on such questions, treating them as trivial. We do not appreciate how finding an answer might affect the outcome of our teaching. Yet if we are going to change the way we teach, if we are going to advance our teaching as we advance our research, then we need to find answers to questions about our teaching and our students' learning. We need to "reflect" on our teaching. One way to begin asking these questions, which may not come to mind readily, is to imitate questions that our students ask us. To do that, we must first listen, really listen, to our students' questions. This can be a novel experience. Here is how I began the process, though with no design to improve my teaching.

By now you know that I always gave the students a long list of assigned reading. And you also know that from the beginning of my teaching days, students complained about the length of the list. Finally, I cut the list almost in half, with regret because I had put considerable effort into selecting the material on the list. I took pride in that reading list. I included a few fundamental papers that were basic to understanding the field, discovery papers, methods papers, papers with recent findings, and several papers that bridged to other disciplines—all in all a robust framework of information for the students "to learn about." To discover another paper to add to the list was a joy, for I was offering the students that much more understanding, or so I thought, except that I wasn't thinking. I was collecting. That was the source of my joy, for as Repplier (1931/1971) remarked, "There is no keener satisfaction in this world than the satisfaction of the collector" (p. 160).

Then one Thursday after the special class, two students and I were sitting on lab benches, chatting across the aisle about various topics. In the informal atmosphere of the special class I would be asked about such matters as the nature of graduate school, which I had never been asked about in a lecture classroom. Anyway, we were chatting away when one of the students calmly asked me, "Why do you have such a long reading list? We don't do all the reading." My first reaction was, "Why is this student talking to me like this?" I was shocked, hurt, disappointed. For goodness sake, I had cut the darn list in half, already. And they still didn't read all the papers? But I sat there and listened. For the first time I, the teacher, listened to a student explain a deficiency in my (vague) learning expectations.

In the nonthreatening environment of the special class and the neighboring time right before and after that class, she obviously felt free to ask me such a question and to justify it. Just as obviously, she did not feel free to ask it during or after lecture period. Although I felt freed from the risks associated with the lecture hall, I had not expected students to feel so. The student who had posed the question was no dummy. She was one of the best students in the school. I respected her. Later she received a graduate fellowship in national competition. She spoke with such honesty and such trust in me that the question struck home. Puzzled and saddened, I asked myself, "Why are we at such odds?"

In this way I discovered that although in the special class I had indeed fled the risk of the lecture, I had come face to face with the risk of free conversation with students. While it may be presumptuous of me, I like to think of this risk as the one Palmer (1998) mentions as a gift of good teachers, the risk "of inviting open dialogue, though I can never know where it is going" (p. 69). All I know for sure is that from then on, I paid closer attention to the topics students talked to me about that had little to do with the lesson for a Thursday. I learned that students were concerned not only with what graduate school was like, but with why they never heard in their classes about using their science to do "useful" or "helpful" things, and with when they would finally get a job and stop living "like a student." In short, for the first time in my years of teaching I was getting to know my students as young men and women with questions, hopes, and concerns about the present and future. But let's go back to what turned out for my teaching career to be a critical question.

The two students told me that they didn't read all the papers on the reading list because they didn't have the time. Now, if that had been the only reason given, I would have been disappointed in them for using such a flimsy excuse. We all have the same 24 hours in the day. It's how we use those hours that differs. But being good students, they had, for them, a solid reason for not using their time to read all the papers. They said they didn't need to, because not all the papers were referred to in class or on the exams. But didn't they find the papers interesting? Well, no, several of the papers, being journal articles, were difficult for them to understand. Other papers were on aspects of the topic that simply didn't interest them. The truth of their simple, honest statements startled me. The implications further saddened me, for if top students, such as these two, didn't read the papers, then students with less ability must not be reading them either. And if most of the class did not read the papers and if I had never failed a student for not reading the papers, then reading the papers was not required for passing the course. So what was the purpose of the reading list, after all? Suddenly, I didn't know. That is what critically reflecting on your teaching can get you. A big, fat I don't know. But it does clear the air.

This feedback from the students disturbed me because their opinions about the reading list must represent a general opinion, and that set me to thinking—or reflecting—for some time. I couldn't just shrug off the question, for there was something about talking face to face with the students that so stamped the matter with importance as to require me to seek answers. Was the problem me? Or was it the students? Was my reading list different from the lists of other instructors? Were my students different? How would I find the answers?

The feedback disturbed me all the more because the second student acknowledged that she had difficulty learning from reading. And she was a senior. That she placed such trust in me as to tell me of her problem humbled me. I felt so sorry for her. And I felt helpless and confused. Throughout all my years of teaching, I was so intent on transmitting content to students that I would have declared it impossible for a senior in university to have had difficulty learning from reading. But there she sat. Although I didn't know what I could do for her before the term was over, I was worried that other students must suffer from the same handicap to their learning. Surely it was my responsibility to help future students in the class, but I was pondering something that had nothing to do with what I knew, the content of the course. I was at a loss. I didn't know how to help them improve their reading, but I felt I had to do something about both the reading and the reading list.

Seeking Answers

I now know that there are five ways to seek answers to questions arising from student feedback: 1) Bring up the matter for discussion with your students, 2) ask a colleague, 3) ask a consultant at the teaching center at your institution, 4) go to the education literature, or 5) do your own research. Back then my choices were fewer. I did not discuss the matter with my students because, being still content bound, I did not want to take time away from a Thursday special class and I felt that I could not take time away from covering the content in lecture class. (If you do discuss a matter like this with your students, be sure you know how you will seek to understand their argument and not open the discussion defensively.) I did ask a colleague, though. He complained that the students did not read the papers he assigned, either. To my misfortune, I was neither aware that the teaching center existed nor familiar with the education literature. So I did my own research.

My hypothesis was that if undergraduate students in my discipline at other universities held the same opinions as my students about assigned reading and other issues of undergraduate education, then my students were not an anomaly. To draw out the opinions of students elsewhere would mean my going there to make an anecdotal survey of opinion, but I was not a researcher in education. My Ph.D. was not in education; I had written no papers on education, given no talks; I had not a single credential to warrant anyone permitting me to converse with their students. This absence of credentials petrified me. More than once I considered forgetting about the whole thing. Yet I couldn't ignore the problem. I decided to write letters to the chairs of departments—almost all strangers to me—at 12 universities, asking if I might come and listen to their students. (Writing that sentence was easy; writing those letters was agony. Talk about feeling like an imposter!) If not courage, it certainly took gumption.

While I waited for replies, assuming my letters would not be dismissed out of hand, the risk I had taken continually burst into my thoughts. At bottom, I felt there was the possibility that my credibility in scientific research might suffer from my posing as a researcher in education. My only consolation was that I had been teaching for years, and experience ought to count for something as a basis for my actions. Well, as it turned out, my anxiety was needless: 10 departments welcomed me; the chairs were gracious; the students forthcoming and forthright; the opinions pretty much the same wherever I went.

With respect to the assigned reading, students read the papers that the instructor or grapevine told them would be on the exam. We can rant and rave that our students ought to be as interested in what we teach them as we are, but they are not the expert learner in the field that we are. So many of the courses they take are perceived as hurdles to jump over on the way to their degree that they husband their interest while in them in order to spend it on courses that naturally interest them or courses in which the instructor engages their interest. Even in those courses they will manage their time to fit their own priorities. We need to engage their interest as novice learners in our field, to motivate them (Davis, 1993, Motivating Students; McKeachie, 2002, Motivation in the College Classroom). We must engage them "at the level of their original motivation" (Palmer, 1998, p. 127) when they entered our discipline.

I also heard from faculty in department after department that their students did not know how to learn by reading. The students would use highlighters to mark sentences or make photocopies of pages in the readings and then assume that looking at the text somehow translated into understanding the meaning. Now I knew I had to do something for my students. Once more I was sticking my nose into an issue that was not derived from the content of my discipline, but by the time the fall term arrived I had come upon the classic book by Adler and Van Doren (1972), *How to Read a Book*, and abstracted from it a handout for my students to guide them in reading for understanding. It was a crude attempt to help them, but I never thought to go to the next step, which is to help them learn to read in the discipline. In a survey of "the best college teachers," Bain (2004) "found among the most effective teachers a strong desire to help students learn to read in the discipline" (p. 56) and he mentions some of the methods they used to accomplish that. You can begin helping your students by applying those and other recommendations (Davis, 1993, Motivating Students to Do the Reading; McKeachie, 2002, How Do You Get Students to Do the Assigned Reading?; Nilson, 2003, Getting Your Students to Do the Readings).

My visits had provided me with answers to the questions raised by the students and to the questions that those questions had generated in my mind. The answers excited me, and being an academic, I wanted to share that excitement with my colleagues. Had the answers been to questions raised in the process of research in my discipline, I would have known precisely how to share them. But these answers pertained to issues secluded within the privacy of my classroom. The faculty in my department had never talked about teaching, at least substantively. Never had a faculty meeting been devoted to teaching and learning. I had no reason to think the faculty would be interested in what I had discovered, but I really wanted to let people know about it.

One action I knew how to take from my years in scientific research was to write a manuscript about the results of my visits. After completing the manuscript, I asked several of my students to review it, which they did, with constructive criticism. Then I was faced with the problem of finding a journal that would consider it for publication.

It always amazes me how limited our power of observation is. Now that I had information I wanted to share with other faculty, I began to observe announcements of educational journals in my discipline and in broader disciplines that included mine. The announcements had been

there all along. I had paid them no attention because they did not interest me, but now that I had a need to know, they engaged my interest.
(That student interest in my class could likewise be engaged by a need to
know sailed right over my head.) I also noticed an announcement in the
newsletter of a professional society in my discipline: a meeting was to be
held in a few months to discuss undergraduate education in the Earth sciences, which includes my discipline of oceanography. This announcement was a call for papers. Well, I certainly had something to say. The
people attending that meeting and presenting papers would be interested
in education. I had discovered an audience for my findings, and, unbe-
knownst to me, the experience would change my life in the classroom.

All I needed was the money to get me to The Meeting, which, would-
n't you know, was in Washington, DC, clear across the country. I gathered my thoughts, arranged my findings for presentation at The Meeting,
and with gnawing anxiety went to see the director of the school to request
some travel funds. The very thought of asking for funds to travel to an
education meeting when, as faculty, we were already educators, had been
teaching for years, nay, decades, and had never had to spend a single day
learning how to teach—well, that just about exhausted the rest of my
gumption. But the director was very supportive. He gave me the funds,
and I went to The Meeting that September. It was to begin with a reception on Wednesday evening and end at noon Sunday, three and a half
days of sessions.

The announcement stated that "The Meeting is composed of oral
and poster presentations." I had presented many papers at scientific
meetings in my discipline. The oral papers were normally ten-to-twelve
minute lectures with five or three minutes at the end for discussion. The
posters were set up for a morning or afternoon with the presenter expected to be on hand for all, or a definite part, of the time to discuss the paper
with passersby. Surely this meeting would be no different.

My abstract accepted, I was already practicing my talk, for I had indicated on the abstract that I preferred to give an oral presentation, when
five days before The Meeting an email message arrived from the co-chairs
of the session in which my paper was scheduled. In the first paragraph
they wrote that they "would like to fill [me] in a bit more on the schedule," a courtesy I greatly appreciated. Then I read that I was one of eight

presenters in the session, each of whom would have two or three minutes to present the main points of his or her paper. I gasped. Two or three minutes! How fast did they expect me to talk? The message continued: Following the talks and a coffee break, the presenters would lead an hour and fifteen minutes of "concurrent interactive presentations and discussions" at their posters. That the talk would be only two minutes and that I would also have to prepare a poster was shock enough, but I hadn't the foggiest notion what an "interactive presentation" was. Oh, lordy, what had I got myself into?

The Meeting

On Wednesday I flew to DC, settled in at the huge hotel a couple of blocks from the headquarters of the professional society that was hosting The Meeting, and made my way there for the evening registration and opening reception. When I walked into the reception room, I stopped dead. A hundred people were wandering about comfortably or grouped in animated conversations, nibbling hors d'oeuvres, sipping wine, everyone seeming to know one another, and within that merry room I recognized nary a face. When I went to a meeting in my discipline, I knew many of the people, had known some of them for years, and was familiar with their work. But here! I stood rooted to the carpet. Why in heaven's name had I thought I belonged here? I was stripped bare: a novice. No, a mere amateur! Before I could self-degrade to a lowly tyro, I aimed myself toward the haven of the hors d'oeuvres table, where I could stand and pretend to study the now-unappetizing selection.

Before the evening was over, another 50 people had arrived, and I had at least become acquainted with a few people. Most important, I had come to appreciate the significance underlying the trivial observation that aspects of education cut across disciplines. The people in the room turned out to be specialists in geology, geophysics, atmospheric science, engineering, or oceanography; from research universities, master's universities, liberal arts colleges, federal government agencies, state government agencies, professional societies, educational associations, museums, consulting companies, or science book publishers. What drew us there was not our highly varied professional specialties but simply an interest in education, a far deeper interest than I had previously held or known to be held by other faculty. (In the future I would discover that one of the thrills of attending an education meeting was the diversity of discipline specialties brought to it by the participants. That evening the diversity was anything but thrilling.)

Back in the hotel I got ready for bed but couldn't sleep. A co-chair of my session the next morning had explained to me the nature of that session. After the two-minute talks and the coffee break, we would spend the time at our posters pretty much as for any poster session. Meanwhile, four of the chairs and conveners would roam the room to collect ideas for the plenary part of the session to follow, in which a few resolutions, recommendations, and observations were to be proposed for the report of The Meeting. These decisions would be revisited on the Sunday morning wrap-up session.

I had never heard of a session structured like this. There was so much talking among people. At sessions of my discipline, you sat in your chair and listened silently to the presenter's lecture. Then a couple of questions would be asked. What was wrong with that? You made a few notes on the program in your lap and had learned something. And at the poster sessions no one roamed around taking notes for a get-together by the presenters. Lying there, staring into the darkness, I was not at all eager to greet the dawn of a new day.

After brief welcoming talks, the morning session began with the keynote speech, by the director of a federal agency that hired students in the disciplines represented at The Meeting. He spoke perceptively on the topics The Meeting was to address: curriculum content, curriculum materials, pedagogy, institutional and faculty changes, public and K–12 education, partnerships and collaborations, and distribution of the results reached at The Meeting. So many of the points that he made were about ideas, observations, needs, and relationships I had never heard of that they whirled round and round in my head with no place for attachment to anything I already knew. Welcome to a talk about education! I had to chuckle ruefully at the thought I had long held that there was nothing intellectual to teaching; it was just something you did.

After a few questions and answers that made uncomfortably clear to me his talk had been understood by most of the people around me, the first of two focus papers was presented. I had never heard of a focus paper. They set the stage for the theme of this session. They also contained several points about students and careers that I had never thought about. Then came the first of the eight two-minute speakers. I was the second; I rose; I spoke; I sat down. And soon we had the coffee break. If I had any coffee, I don't remember it. I wanted to find the bulletin board for my poster in the large room, and I wanted to be alone.

While pinning my sheets of paper to the bulletin board, I kept turning over in my mind the content of my poster and trying desperately to keep out all thoughts of how little I understood of what I had heard the other speakers say. I felt like a visitor in a different world. It was a blessing when the poster part of the session began, because I could concentrate entirely on discussing with people the findings of my visit to the 10 departments. In spite of the exception taken by a couple of people to one or two of my findings, I enjoyed talking about my findings, just as I always enjoyed talking about my research results in my discipline, and I received some helpful suggestions about interpreting my findings. By the end of the poster part of the session I had gained a little confidence that I belonged there. Then everyone returned to the lecture room, where the two co-chairs and two focus speakers presented bulleted starting points taken from their observations of the discussions during the poster period and from the text of our submitted abstracts. In the ensuing group discussion, some recommendations and observations were drawn that the group concluded should be in the report of The Meeting. Finally, at lunch I could relax a bit, because my presentation was finished.

The afternoon session, on undergraduate curriculum, was structured differently from the morning session. The three co-chairs each gave a 15-minute focus paper, the first of which so amazed me that I took more notes on it than on any other paper, including the keynote address. The speaker was a faculty member from a small elite liberal arts college. In describing his department he spoke of there being lots of group work in class, lots of writing, lots of speaking, class presentations, research in all courses, a noncompetitive and informal environment, a department atmosphere that was more important than the curriculum. I had never heard of such a department. I didn't know what to make of it, but I was intrigued. Perhaps in some ways it was an elegant echo of my liberal arts undergraduate days.

Instead of poster presentations, this session was divided into five breakout groups, and I found myself tagging along to my first breakout group. I took a seat with other members of the breakout group around the edge of a room and listened to the discussion, more than participated in it. It seemed to me that almost every aspect of curriculum that was raised had never been discussed in meetings of the faculty in my school. I had taught for years in a research university without ever being part of a fundamental discussion of curriculum. The objective of the breakout discussion was to arrive at recommendations and observations and to report back to the plenary part of the session at the end of the day. There, the reports of the five breakout group leaders formed the basis for a discussion to prepare a list of recommendations and observations on undergraduate curriculum for the report of The Meeting. The conference dinner at the hotel brought a full, tiring day to a close for me. In my room, I relived the small joy of telling people about my findings—and the overwhelming fatigue from my ignorance of education, which had been regularly exposed.

The sessions for the next two days were variations on the structure of the sessions for the first day. I had resigned myself to being a part of the activity, instead of sitting and listening to lectures, but not a very active part, because I felt I didn't know enough to be active. One switch from lecture really annoyed me. It happened this way. The speaker was standing at the overhead projector and had commented about the topic. Then, instead of telling us the conclusion, he told us to turn to the person sitting next to us and discuss what the conclusion might be. Dumbfounded, I looked at that young man and wondered what in the hell was the matter with him. He already knew the answer. Why didn't he just tell us the answer and get on with it? Why play games with us? Perhaps he was joking. But no! Oh, no! He was serious. I stole a peek at the fellow sitting next to me and thought, "If he knows no more about this than I do, we are in deep trouble." As it turned out, however, he knew a lot more than I did, but that didn't ameliorate my irritation at the lecturer's shirking his responsibility.

One of the two-minute talks on the last afternoon was about a topic that had little relevance to my course, but the presenter also mentioned the method she used to teach the course. The method sounded strange; undetected, it bored deep into my memory. It was called a "jigsaw," a form of cooperative learning that was created by Aronson, Blaney, Stephan, Sikes, and Snapp (1978) for students working in groups. Each group of students was assigned a reading or activity that supplied part of the information needed to achieve the goal for that class lesson. After demonstrating to the instructor that they knew the material, the groups were reformed into mixed groups, each consisting of a member from each of the original groups. Each member of the mixed groups then taught the other members what that student's group had learned, thus combining the information from all the original groups so as to achieve the goal for the class lesson. The instructor caught any mistakes or oversights.

Like the man who had mentioned group work earlier, she was also from a small elite liberal arts college. At her poster part of the session, she had a five-page handout that described how to structure the course for the jigsaw format of cooperative learning. I picked up a copy and glanced at it with a strange ambivalence—perhaps "strange" because I cannot profess to have associated what intrigued me about this example of group work with my discomfort at participating in group work during The Meeting. (How easily we ignore contradictions!) I had a couple of questions, which she seemed very happy to answer. I walked away holding the handout and with an obscure agitation deep inside me. Little did I know that by taking that handout I had advanced to Stage 1 in the stages of concern about innovative teaching (see Table 4.1): I had wanted to know more about the innovation. It was a small step in itself, totally unappreciated by me as the significant behavioral expression that it was of my development as a teacher. (For a discussion of faculty development in teaching, see Biggs, 1999; Hebert & Loy, 2002; Nyquist & Wulff, 1996; and Weimer, 2002.)

Table 4.1

Stages of Concern: Typical Expressions of Concern About the Innovation

Nature of Concern	Stages of Concern	Expressions of Concern
Impact	6. Refocusing	I have some ideas about something that would work even better.
	5. Collaboration	I am concerned about relating what I am doing with what other instructors are doing.
	4. Consequence	How is my use affecting kids?
Task	3. Management	I seem to be spending all my time getting material ready.
Self	2. Personal	How will using it affect me?
	1. Informational	I would like to know more about it.
	0. Awareness	I am not concerned about it (the innovation).

Note. From *Taking Charge of Change* by S. M. Hord, W. L. Rutherford, L. Huling-Austin, and G. E. Hall, 1987, Austin, TX: Southwest Educational Development Laboratory. Copyright 1987 by the Southwest Educational Development Laboratory. All rights reserved. Reprinted with permission.

At the Sunday morning wrap-up session, I was introduced to yet another method of group work. In informal groups of three to five, we were asked to make recommendations and observations about the seven topics that had defined The Meeting, based on summaries of the conclusions already reached in the sessions. Sheets of butcher paper were stuck on the walls of the large room under each of the topics. As each small group decided on a recommendation or observation for a topic, someone from the group was to take a marker and write it on the appropriate sheet of paper on the wall. These sheets would provide the conveners with final comments from the participants. In this activity I participated fully, although I considered it a strange way to obtain information.

I left my first education meeting and took the shuttle to the airport, vaguely pleased, considerably perplexed, and still deeply agitated. I was pleased that I had survived The Meeting and had learned about so many different aspects of undergraduate teaching and learning. The pleasure was tempered by perplexity, both the perplexity at my astonishing lack of knowledge about teaching, despite having taught for more years than most of the participants at The Meeting, and the perplexity at being an awkward and ineffective member of the variously structured discussion groups, and I have not mentioned all of the structures I encountered. Underlying these surface feelings lay an obscure agitation.

Reflective Questions

- *Can you remember a question about your teaching that a student asked you?*

- *How might you have answered it better?*

- *How can you provide students more opportunities to talk to you?*

- *What question about your teaching would you like most to have answered?*

- *Whom can you approach to help you answer that question?*

- *Which of my reactions to The Meeting do you share?*

- *Why is it so difficult for us to be a novice learner?*

- *To what extent is the difficulty the same for the students in our classes?*

5

CHANGE ALTERS WHAT YOU PUT INTO THE COURSE

Daring to Do It

I took the 5:20 p.m. nonstop flight from Dulles to Seattle. Gradually the world outside the window vanished into the darkness behind me. Ever so often I punched on the overhead reading light, slid my briefcase from under the seat, and took out that five-page handout on the jigsaw structure for cooperative learning. I wasn't aware that the vague internal agitation had surfaced in nervous activity. I would reread the handout, tuck it back into the briefcase for a while, only to haul it out again. It still seemed the darnedest way to teach a class I had ever heard of. And yet, perhaps it allowed me to picture what the speaker who had described the enticing department atmosphere at his liberal arts college had had in mind. I had certainly been intrigued by his description of the classes, particularly the students working in groups, but couldn't figure out how he had set the class up to teach it like that. Now I was holding a procedure that showed me one way it might be done.

I had reached Stage 2, the personal stage, in the stages of concern about innovation (as shown earlier in Table 4.1): How would using the jigsaw affect me? What should I do first? I cannot say that I harbored doubts of my success. The more often I read it, the more enticing the idea became until, by the time I landed in Seattle, I had decided to try the jigsaw form of cooperative learning in my course. (Okay, okay, two martinis and wine with dinner at 35,000 feet would probably make any new teaching method look good.)

When I sat in my office the next morning, staring at the leaning stack of lecture notes and the untidy lot of overhead transparencies for the course, I knew I had to do it. I simply couldn't face another term of wading through those notes and overheads. Later I learned that this was not the best way to select a teaching method. Rather, I should first have come to know my students, perhaps even to gain some understanding of the mental habits that underlay their motivations and learning styles (Lawrence, 1982), and then set learning outcomes or goals for them; that is to say, what I wanted them to learn and be able to do with that learning (Davis, 1993, Syllabus; McKeachie, 2002, Syllabus; Weimer, 2002, Techniques). That would have prepared me to select the teaching method best suited to achieve those outcomes for those students.

The goals or learning outcomes are the results I want to achieve. That is, they are where I want the students and me to be, which tells me where the students and I are now, and the teaching method is the form of activity I'll use to move the students in such a manner as to achieve those results (Covey, 1990). Not knowing that, I went about it the wrong way round. But I had a darn good reason for doing so: Fall term began in two weeks. If I was really going to stick my neck out and change my teaching, I had to bull ahead. There was no time to reflect on my teaching. In fact, it's possible that had I stopped to reflect, I would have spent all my time reflecting and had to postpone the act of making the change until the next year—or even later.

The first task was to change the stack of lecture notes into student activities. I wished for a magic wand but settled for making the change this way: I looked at the outline of the course from the previous term. For each day Monday through Wednesday two or three topics were listed for the lecture. Thursday, remember, was the special class period. For each topic I had pages of neatly written notes and way too many overhead transparencies of figures, graphs, maps, and other illustrations. The lecture notes, probably like yours, were condensed compilations of information taken from various books and journals, many of which were too advanced for these students to be expected to read for understanding.

The topics for the first two lectures were aspects of a natural process and those for the next three lectures were aspects of the natural response to that process. I decided to find textbooks or reference books that covered these topics at a level the students could understand, all the while reminding myself of the difficulty that students have in reading for understanding. There are, of course, other ways to use reading materials (Meyers & Jones, 1993, Integrating Reading Materials), and there are other kinds of materials to use for a jigsaw, such as data, samples, case studies, experiments, or demonstrations.

I also had to know how much reading material to look for. On being told that 20 students had enrolled in the course, I decided to divide them into five groups of four students for the jigsaw structure. Therefore, I had to find five readings for each topic, one for each group, and the readings had to overlap sufficiently in content so that when the students moved into the mixed groups, the information in the readings could be connected together by the students, with guidance from my focus questions. (For other suggestions about using the jigsaw structure, as well as additional references, see Aronson, Blaney, Stephan, Sikes, & Snapp, 1978; Clarke, 1994; and Millis & Cottell, 1998, Jigsaw; see online Aronson, 2000.)

Selecting the readings consumed far more time than I had expected. This was my first woeful underestimation of the time required for this mode of teaching. More would come. I had now left behind sole emphasis on self-concerns about the innovation and entered Stage 3, management concerns ("I seem to be spending all my time getting material ready"), where I would remain for much of the term (see Table 4.1 shown earlier). Most material was too advanced, too elementary, or too specialized. Finally, for the first topic, the natural process, I found two textbooks that were appropriate. The reading for each group was only two to six pages long. The focus question for them to answer dealt with a significant point in the reading; for instance, one group might be asked about some characteristics of the process whereas another group would be asked about other characteristics of the process or characteristics of the process under different conditions. The short reading and a focus question to be answered seemed a feasible assignment for the students to complete by the following day.

Creating those focus questions propelled me rudely into contemplating what I wanted my students to learn, for the questions served as a structure to guide the students in their reading and learning. To set the stage for a topic, I was supposed to tell the students what they were expected to learn and be able to do with that learning (Davis, 1993, Syllabus; McKeachie, 2002, Goals; Weimer, 2002, Function of Content). As you might expect, I still couldn't carry this off very well, but I was improving. How many times up to this point have you read that I wanted my students "to know about" the material? That could mean anything. I was still teaching innocently: "Teaching innocently means thinking that we're always understanding exactly what it is that we're doing and what effect we're having" (Brookfield, 1995, p. 1). I had always assumed that students would somehow divine what was expected of them. Now, however, I realized that I had to let them know what was important—but there was little time for me to ponder that challenge. The first day of class was rushing at me. (By the second year, I improved the questions, the better to guide the students toward what I wanted them to learn. Don't give up if your first attempt at any part of the change falls short.)

To my surprise—just the first—and disappointment, the first reading assignment covered only part of the content that I had covered in my first day of lecture. By the time I had found readings to cover the main points of what I had lectured about on the natural process—not everything I had lectured about for two days, you understand, just the main points as tagged by the focus questions—I had four reading assignments (a total of four assignments times five groups for twenty different readings) and a nagging premonition that I was taking too long on the topic. But I was committed. So, on I plunged. In hindsight, I was learning how adaptable and flexible you have to be when having the students take an active role in their learning. And I was learning it fast, as a fumbling novice. But "just looking ahead was becoming exciting" (Covey, 1990, p. 63).

I don't believe long days have ever flown by in a shorter time. Suddenly it was the first day of class. I was anxiously standing in front of 24 students—not 20, so there was an adjustment to make—ready to tell them about the course they had registered for with the expectation that it would be a typical lecture course. (Expectation? A few years later a student from that class told me that she had asked a student who had taken the course the year before, "What is Dean's course like?" and had been told, "It's a snoozer." There you have it—what the students sitting in the lecture hall that day were expecting—a snoozer.) Well, the five-page handout from the meeting said to take time on the first day of class to explain to the students how the course would be taught and why, and what I expected of them. And that's what I spent the entire 50 minutes doing (see Brown, 2000, The Challenge of Preparation).

What would I like for them to learn? Two things. Beginning with number two, I said, "Second most important: some marine geology [and I showed them some 35mm slides of shoreline features while commenting on the features. I had done this in past years. But then I said something new.] In particular, I want you to gain enough understanding of what's going on at a beach to be able to advise the uninformed person and to predict possible results of changes in processes. Though not an expert, you should have some idea of what should be done to preserve the beach and you should be able to communicate that idea to the public. The most important thing to learn, however, is certain skills."

That short paragraph from my lecture notes holds a lot of meaning. I finally say that I want them to learn "this," enough understanding of beach processes, to do "that," communicate that knowledge and make predictions. My emphasis is still on their being able to do something with what they learn but now it is not fashioned as future employment. The only learning outcome stated, though still vaguely, pertains to the part of the course for which I had already selected readings and written focus questions. This is what happens when you begin to think more about what you want the students to get out of the course than what information you are going to put into the course. About the rest of the course, I had nothing to say, the same naive silence as in years past. The implication, of course, as always, is "learn everything," impossible though that is.

I paused in my talk to the students. It was now time to get down to details, and if you think I was anxious, you're darn right. But it was the excited anxiety of commencing something I wanted to do rather than the gnawing anxiety of dreading something I had to do. I took a deep breath and said, "This course will probably be like no other course you have had. There will be no exams." My heart was racing. The polite attention on the students' faces dissolved into astonishment. Startled glances darted about. I said bravely, "And there will be no lectures. You will work together in groups." My heart pounded louder. I leaned against the lectern for support. The students froze, wide-eyed.

Only after the course was over did I learn how threatened many of them felt by these words, especially the best students. For they knew how to play the system, how to take good notes, how to cram for exams, and here I had just changed the system. I was threatening their ability to get good grades. One 4.0 student later told me, "If your course hadn't been required, I would have dropped it that first day." This unsolicited feedback not only helped me improve as a teacher but it was an act of partnership that improved the course. For it enabled me on the first day of class the next year to try to allay the students' anxieties about their grades.

You may well think it irresponsible of me not to have anticipated the students' anxiety. After all, when I was thrown into active learning just as heartlessly at The Meeting, I felt threatened. My empathy should have overflowed for them, but it didn't. All I can say is that my anxiety as instructor must have captured my attention and feelings. Or to put it bluntly: I was thinking only of myself—what I had to do. I reverted back to the personal Stage 2 of concerns about innovation (shown earlier in Table 4.1), "How will using it affect me?" rather than rising to Stage 4, the consequence stage, "How is my use affecting kids [students]?" (Incidentally, Table 4.1 was written for elementary school teachers, who refer to their students as "kids." I have never thought of my undergraduates as "kids.")

In my evolutionary development as a teacher I was still at an early stage in which I was not yet sufficiently confident in what I was doing to think about how it might affect the students. No faculty member in my department had ever done what I was about to do in that class: have students work in groups rather than listen to a lecture. My words to the students sounded a lot braver than I felt. It was not so much that I feared failing but that I was trying to remember what to do and how to say it. For some reason, which I could not explain at the time, I truly believed that what I was doing was right, deeply believed it, and that gave me strength and fueled my excitement, but believing it did not make the task any easier.

Never before had students been so engrossed in what I had to say from the lectern. I described for them the format of the course. There would be five groups of four or five students, the members of the groups to be self-selected. (I'll get to the rest of the format in a bit.) And then, very important, I told them why I was using the format. First, research indicated that people learned better by taking an active role in their learning (Bransford, Brown, & Cocking, 1999; Davis, 1993, *Helping Students Learn*; McKeachie, 2002, *Teaching Students How to Learn*;

Weimer, 2002, Lessons on Learning). To be precise, I should say I told them that as best as I could at the time, having next to no knowledge of how people learned. Second, I told them that employers complained that new employees didn't know how to work together in teams, communicate effectively orally or in writing, or carry a project through to completion. (I'm citing no reference here; just pick up almost any newspaper or newsmagazine that has an education section.)

These were some of the skills I wanted the students to learn or polish in this course, but it never entered my mind that it was my responsibility to help them learn how to work together in groups or complete a project; for example, that I should specify the behavior I desired, such as accepting and supporting one another, that I should ensure they knew how to participate in a discussion constructively and resolve disputes constructively, and that I should make sure they knew how to listen (Brown, 2000, Organizing and Guiding; Davis, 1993, Organizing Learning Groups; Johnson, Johnson, & Smith, 1991, Basic Elements of Cooperative Learning; Meyers & Jones, 1993, Structuring Groups for Success). Once again I forgot my discomfort and timid participation in the group activities at The Meeting. I naively believed that all I had to do was have the students get together in groups and they would know what to do.

My ignorance of the responsibility to set the stage and prepare the students for group work is probably mirrored by most faculty who have only lectured. A TA once told me that the professor in her course would tell her, "We're supposed to do group work, so have the students do something for class tomorrow." How about you? When you took the Teaching Goals Inventory, following Chapter 2, did your goals cluster only in "Higher-Order Thinking Skills" and "Discipline-Specific Knowledge and Skills"? Those are not the skills required for successful group work.

Although the students grouped themselves together naturally, as I had seen other students do in my Thursday special classes, the groups they were forming here were different, more formal, and the students told me that they had not worked in groups like this before. The only skills I recognized having a responsibility to help them learn to use were speaking and writing, for these were the skills that I already knew something about how to teach. As we'll see, the performance of some students in their groups would be handicapped by my ignorance.

I went on to tell them about the projects they would undertake, the grading system, and my office hours. Although I also said they would be co-teachers of the course, I would have been more accurate had I said they would assist me in the teaching, for they truly did assist me. And I emphasized how essential their attendance would be. If they were absent, they would let their group down. Attendance turned out to be far better with cooperative learning than it had ever been with lecturing, when one-third of the class would be absent on any given day. (It dawned on me that since I had never failed one-third of the class, they obviously had not needed to be present every day in order to pass the course. My self-esteem thanked me for not having recognized this insult to my lecturing while I was teaching by lecturing, for I would have had no solution to the absences but to give pop quizzes to force attendance—a pitiful act of desperation.)

Then I had the students select their groups. Cooperative learning consists of wonderful variety and flexibility. There are other ways to form groups than by letting the students self-select (Johnson et al., 1991, Preinstructional Decisions; Millis & Cottell, 1998, Team Formation; Stein & Hurd, 2000, Some Basic Configurations of Teams), just as there are other structures for cooperative learning besides the jigsaw (Millis & Cottell, 1998, Beginning Structures). And don't forget, there are other forms of active learning (Davis, 1993, Collaborative Learning, Role Playing, Supplements and Alternatives to Lectures; McKeachie, 2002, Active Learning, Problem Based Learning).

Once the hubbub had died down and the groups had been formed, I passed out the assignment for the next day. Each student was to read the assigned reading, answer the focus question, and type a one-page answer to the question—double spaced, because I wanted them to learn to be concise. One copy of the answer was to be handed in to me the next day at the beginning of class; the second copy was for their reference as their group discussed the answer. By making an assignment on the first day of class to be turned in the next day, I had set the pace for the course immediately. Without my telling them, they knew right away that they would be working in this course. And thus did the first day of class come to an end.

Preparing to Work in Groups

The first day of class is indeed the most important day of the term (Bain, 2004, What Big Questions Will My Course Help Students Answer . . . ?; Davis, 1993, First Day of Class; Grunert, 1997; McKeachie, 2002, Meeting for the First Time; Nilson, 2003, Your First Day of Class; Stein & Hurd, 2000, On Your Mark). It's very easy not to assign it that importance, even though how we begin the course can determine how it will run. If we make the first day a throwaway day, we should not be surprised if students call the course a throwaway course. In later years I learned that my actions that first day, though appropriate as far as they went, didn't go far enough. For instance, this is when I could have led a discussion about working in groups (Millis & Cottell, 1998, Establishing Classroom Norms; Race, 2000, Establishing Ground Rules for Groups).

When I later read about the interpersonal skills required for successful group work (Brown, 2000, Developing Student Expertise; Johnson et al., 1991, Basic Elements of Cooperative Learning; Meyers & Jones, 1993, Cooperative Student Projects; Stein & Hurd, 2000, Criteria for Successful Teamwork), I was amazed that the students in my first attempt had been so successful with such little guidance from me. I was very proud of them, and I was very fortunate that they were mature young men and women, seniors, and majors in my discipline. Had I been dealing with freshman or sophomore nonmajors, I might well have had my hands full with personal problems among students.

Or had my students been more racially or ethnically diverse, my ignorance of inclusive teaching might have hampered their learning (Wlodkowski & Ginsberg, 2003). Nevertheless, active learning techniques, with their emphasis on a community of learners working together and learning from one another, are effective—in the right hands—for use in enhancing learning in today's diverse, or inclusive, classroom (Bain, 2004, Expecting More from Students with Low Grades; Bransford et al., 1999, Classroom and School Communities; Johnson et al., 1991, Interpersonal Attraction and Cohesion; Meyers & Jones, 1993, A Changing Student Body; Millis & Cottell, 1998, The Changing Student Population). In fact, the jigsaw structure was developed by Aronson et al.

(1978) specifically as "an effective instructional technique and a way of integrating our schools" (p. 13) following the U.S. Supreme Court 1954 decision in *Brown v. The Board of Education, Topeka, Kansas.* The results of their field experiments and other studies support its use in the diverse, or inclusive, classroom.

I had left the lectern. Now I was committed. Little did I know how essential my commitment was to the success of this change in my teaching. As I later learned, had I hinted that I was unsure about using cooperative learning, the students could have picked up on that doubt and been more likely to resist the change. So you must enter the change with commitment. It's called leadership—a characteristic that we faculty are more prone to study than exhibit.

Table 5.1 is the outline of the first 10 days of the course. Don't get excited. Faculty tend to look at this outline and declare, "There is no way I could make up an outline like that before a course began." Well, neither did I. I prepared this outline long after the course was over. During the course, I did not know how long it would take the students to complete each step—how long to discuss, how long to teach, and so forth. This uncertainty caused me some anxiety. Also notice that although topics are listed (I had not broken from the tradition of listing topics), emphasis is on the students' activities. So let's see what the students did in these activities.

On the second day of the course we met in the lab that I had used for the Thursday special classes. The students sat on opposite sides of the table-like benches or clustered at the table ends, facing one another. For the rest of the term we met in this room rather than the lecture hall (Meyers & Jones, 1993, Coping with Teaching Space; Johnson et al., 1991, Preinstructional Decisions). In my opinion the best arrangement for group work is a room of round tables for four or five students, because round tables allow uniform eye contact and round tables have no sides, which can divide a group. But I found only one room of round tables in all the institutions I have visited.

The students handed in one copy of their answers to me and kept the other copy to talk from in their group discussions. They could not participate in the discussion if they failed to hand in a copy of their answers. Having them turn in a product, for this lesson a one-page paper, ensured

Table 5.1

Outline of the First Ten Days in the Jigsaw Structure of Cooperative Learning

Day	Topic	Activities	Assignment	Due
1	Intro.	Select groups	Readings 1	
2	Topic 1	5 groups: Discussion		1-page answer to Readings 1
3	Topic 1	4 mixed groups: Teaching		
4	Topic 1	4 mixed groups: Teaching	Synthesis of Readings 1	
5	Topic 2	Problem solving: Groups use different methods	Solve problems in Exercise 1	2-page synthesis of Readings 1
6	Topic 2	Groups teach other groups how to use method to solve problem	Readings 2	Complete Exercise 1
7	Topic 3	5 groups: Discussion		1-page answer to Readings 2
8	Topic 3	4 mixed groups: Teaching		
9	Topic 3	4 mixed groups: Teaching	Synthesis of Readings 2	
10	Computer Lab	Introduction to computer programs for Project 1	Project 1	2-page synthesis of Readings 2

that they completed the assignment; in other words, that they had read the assigned reading. The main purpose of the paper was to help them learn what they had read. The purpose seemed to have been fulfilled, for in the course evaluations at the end of the term, several students wrote much the same as this student: "The 1-page reviews forced me to pick out the most important points. Plus the page restriction helped me to write my points more directly." The students always came to class prepared. No longer was there a problem of not reading the assigned reading. Of course, they could see that the assigned reading was pertinent to understanding the topic. However, I recommend that you read about dealing with unprepared students before the situation arises (Davis, 1993, Encouraging Student Participation; McKeachie, 2002, Problem Students). The best tip I ever received for solving problems of classroom management was to prevent them (see Brown, 2000).

I could have graded those papers. After all, I had read all the assignments; I knew the answers to the focus questions. But I wanted the students to express their knowledge without worrying about a grade. I wanted to see what they got out of the reading. So I read their answers after class, wrote a few constructive comments on the papers, made a note about their performance for my records, and returned the papers the next day. Itemizing my actions like this makes it seem like I spent a lot of time on these papers, but I didn't. I read the papers from the members of a group consecutively since their answers were roughly the same. The note about their performance was a method for me to find out which students were having difficulty with the reading. It is imperative that we give students feedback on their work while they are still interested in being told what they did right and what they did wrong (Davis, 1993, Helping Students Learn; McKeachie, 2002, Motivation). It doesn't take long for that interest to be replaced by an interest solely in the grade, as other assignments take center stage. Our delayed feedback to them, therefore, emphasizes the grade, and grades already receive too much emphasis.

Those first papers revealed much about the students' reading. Most of the answers on the papers were correct and fairly well written. Even though I expected some students would have difficulty reading for understanding, I was nevertheless appalled by some careless mistakes in the answers from a couple of students, mistakes that must have prevented them from understanding the concepts. Had they not been required to write those papers and use that misunderstanding in the group discussion and thereby discover their mistakes, they might have retained their misunderstanding for some time. Of course, my comments on their papers called their attention to the mistakes.

Now, your instinctive reaction may be: "They got the answer wrong. They should be docked some points." Why so? When they met in their groups and began discussing their answers, you can bet these students quickly realized that they had made a mistake, probably to no little embarrassment. Learning always carries a risk with it. In this situation, the risk for the students failing an assignment was "public" embarrassment before their peers, not a "private" bad grade on a returned paper a day later. Which risk would you rate the toughest to deal with? At least before the time came for them to talk to the mixed groups, they could make the corrections in their own groups, where, though embarrassed, they were relatively "safe" with people who had chosen to be together. According to the student evaluations, the main benefit the students derived from the group discussions was the opportunity to clarify confusion from the reading.

What I had put into this course so far was very different from what one puts into a lecture course. I had selected readings, as I had previously selected material from which to write lecture notes, and it took more time, the first time around, to find the readings and make the other changes in the course than it did to write lecture notes the first time. But readings do not have to be selected each term, just as lecture notes do not have to be rewritten each term. In the classroom, my role was to ensure as best I could that the students took out of the course what I wanted them to learn and that they could do with it what I expected. To fulfill that goal is to operate in a variety of roles rather than the one role of lecturer, as we are about to see.

Reflective Questions

- *Select a topic from your lecture notes and read your notes on that topic carefully. What do you really want your students to learn?*

- *What do you want your students to be able to do with that learning?*

- *What publications or authors come to mind that might serve as references your students could read for understanding about this topic?*

- *Where would you look for additional references?*

- *Can you pick two sources and select a passage from each with overlapping content that your students would be able to read for understanding?*

- *What kinds of materials other than readings might you use?*

6

CHANGE EMPHASIZES WHAT STUDENTS TAKE AWAY FROM THE COURSE

Working in Groups

After handing in their papers on that second day, the students staked out their group locations in the lab—and waited hesitantly for what came next. I reminded them of the two objectives of the discussions they were about to begin—to reach a consensus understanding of their answer to the focus question and to prepare to teach it in the mixed groups—told them to have at it, and held my breath behind a smile. I turned my attention on straightening the stack of papers they had handed me. Amid nervous chuckles, much squirming about, and a shuffle of papers, they began their discussions, in low voices.

What did I do then? Well, I walked slowly around the classroom, still nervous about the effect of this new classroom atmosphere on all of us. I had delegated the teaching, as well as the learning, to the students. They would learn it here in the classroom with their peers, where I was available to help them, rather than on their own time after class, as in the lecture format, where I was not available to help them (Walvoord & Anderson, 1998, Rethink the Use of In-Class Time). I was trusting them to accept the responsibility I had delegated to them (Weimer, 2002, Getting Students to Accept the Responsibility for Learning). Would they accept it? I had finally reached Stage 4 of the stages of concern about innovation (see Table 4.1 shown earlier), consequence: How would my use of the jigsaw affect the students?

All instructors know that students don't like to talk about the course material in lecture class. But in this class each student talked from his or her own paper with an answer to the focus question. A greater sense of purpose marked these discussions than discussions in the Thursday special classes. Having that paper to talk from seemed to bolster their confidence. As the students' confidence grew, mine grew too. My nervousness vanished. To hear voices softly discussing the science I loved was heady. (Later in the course, as the students gained yet more confidence in their ability to discuss the material, their voices grew louder—and I grew ecstatic.) At first, groups would fall silent when I stopped beside them. I would tell them, "Go on. Pay no attention to me." Convinced that I wasn't there to quiz them, they would look at one another for a moment and then their discussion would sputter back to life. After about the third class period, they no longer stopped when I paused beside them to listen in on their discussion.

The first objective of the discussion was for the group to reach a consensus on the answer to the focus question. In their course evaluations, several students wrote that their groups helped them to learn, a statement that gratified me greatly. One student wrote, "Interaction with other students created a 'team' spirit. We helped, encouraged, and supported each other in and out of the classroom." Another student wrote, "Reading articles and learning to understand them enough to explain them makes for a great learning experience. Getting the different interpretations of the articles from my peers also increased my understanding of the material."

From student comments like these and my observations, I believe this group spirit is real, not in a sense of competition between groups, although that can be arranged if the instructor wants it (Davis, 1993, Designing Group Work), but, at least in my class, in a sense of support among group members. For this reason, when two students dropped the course (one was an auditor, the other had dropped it before) and I had to move students from other groups to balance the number of members in the groups, the group spirit suffered for the students who were moved.

The most common complaint about the groups was expressed this way by a student: "The group was the best resource, but not if all the members were confused." That confusion was my fault. It was my responsibility to check with each group to make sure they were progressing in their discussion and to make sure their consensus was the correct answer (Johnson, Johnson, & Smith, 1991, Monitoring and Intervening; Weimer, 2002, Do You Intervene, and If So, When?). I did my best at this, but, as a novice learner myself, I was really unprepared. My principal shortcoming, I later realized (and this may strike you as unbelievable), was not knowing how to use questions effectively in discussion (Christensen, 1991; Davis, 1993, Asking Questions). If you wonder how I, a professor who by then had been teaching for more than three decades, could be so unprepared, read on.

I would have fit right in with the majority of mathematics and science instructors in higher education who were surveyed at about that time (Barnes, 1994). This survey reported that instructors used less than 3% of class time in questioning students and that 87% of those questions were at the lowest cognitive level, such as questions to clarify assignments or repeat information. There is little satisfaction, though, in knowing I had plenty of company as an inept questioner. It took me several years to develop even an apprentice's ability. It took practice—the practice of learning a new skill, in this case a workplace skill. Possessing this skill is imperative for an instructor in active learning of any format. It is also essential for the students (Bain, 2004, Questions Are Crucial), but I had not yet realized that, either.

I also needed to learn how to draw out shy students and ensure they benefited from the system. This was another new role for me. One student wrote, "Although Dr. McManus was always open for questions, there were several times I didn't feel comfortable asking for help because I felt I was supposed to be able to figure things out for myself or ask a classmate rather than the instructor." I obviously had not made clear to this student, and probably to others, in what ways I was there to help them. I was a novice in a new practice. I needed time. You will too. Accept those conditions, do the best you can, and learn from them.

There was a great temptation for me to enter into a group's discussion. After all, I already knew a lot about the topic under discussion and could cut to the heart of the matter. But the object was for the students to learn, not for me to tell them the answer. You may recall that in my lecturing days I was only too happy to tell them the answer to a question, for I wanted to help them. Now I was, to the contrary, not telling them the answer, because I wanted to help them. I wanted to help them to think for themselves. I have known instructors using group discussions who find it very difficult not to be the center of attention. Nevertheless, one of the best tips I know for teaching by any form of active learning is to listen to the discussion for mistakes, misunderstandings, confusion, or off-task conversations, and correct or guide them. Otherwise, bite your tongue—it's called *Teaching with Your Mouth Shut* (Finkel, 2000).

The second objective of the group discussion was for the students to decide how they would teach the answer to the mixed groups. Remember that the mixed groups (see Table 5.1 shown earlier) were to be formed of one member from each of the groups. The students knew it was their responsibility as assistant teachers of the course to master the material. By the end of this class period, they were expected to have sufficient command of the material to explain it in their own words to the students from the other groups. It was the knowledge they had gained by the end of class, rather than the knowledge from the reading that they had brought into the class, that was significant—another reason for not spending my time grading the papers they handed in at the beginning of class (Walvoord & Anderson, 1998).

My students took the full 50-minute period to discuss their answers to the questions and decide how they would teach in the mixed groups. (I had guessed it would take them about 20 minutes. Another underestimate of the time required!) We faculty always think it should take our students very little time to learn what we already know. But now I had a class that was progressing at the rate the students were learning, or at least most of the students, instead of at the rate I was delivering information in a lecture. I was beginning to learn about their rate of learning as novices, at least as a group of novices. Discovering their individual rates of learning was, at this stage, merely to be hoped for.

When I say that the students were discussing their answers and then preparing to teach, what I mean is this: Let's say Group A was asked how certain characteristics of a wave, such as its length and height, changed as the wave moved from deep water into shallow water near the shore. The students quickly agreed on what happened to each characteristic as described in the reading (the length decreased, the height increased); then they had to reach an understanding of how the change happened; that is, they had to understand the explanation in the reading. The challenge of how to teach their finding was the same as we face in preparing our lectures. They had to decide what information from the reading was pertinent, how it should be presented, and be as sure as they could be of the accuracy of what they would tell the other students. Meanwhile, the students in Group B were answering the question of how the movement of the particles of water changed as a wave moved from deep water into shallow water. Combining what both groups had learned would enable the students to understand how both the wave form and the water particle motion changed during shoaling and what effect the energy in the wave form had on the motion of the water particles.

As the hands on the wall clock moved toward the time for class to end—and they seemed to move ever faster—I asked each group if they were finished. "No, just a few more minutes," came the answers. But I did manage to squeeze in time to meet with each group and ask, far too superficially, I regret to say, whether they understood the answer and had decided how to teach it. There is a time management problem with this form of teaching: to find the right balance between keeping the course moving and allowing the students sufficient time to discuss the information and plan their teaching (Meyers & Jones, 1993, Managing the Classroom for Small Groups).

Time management was different when I was preparing for a 50-minute lecture. It usually consisted of being sure that I had enough material to fill the time. But with cooperative learning, time management is more complicated. If each student takes, say, a collective 7 minutes to discuss the answer, which is not much time for a novice to express his or her thoughts, and there are 4 or 5 students in the group, that totals 28 to 35 minutes. Then they must plan their teaching. That could take another 15 or 20 minutes, total. Then for me to meet with each of 5 groups would take 50 minutes, for a total of 93 to 105 minutes. By trying to accomplish all this in a 50-minute period I badly rushed my meeting with each group. A 90-minute period is much better for this type of class.

As the term passed, their growing experience made the students more efficient. I improved too. We were all learning new skills, and that takes time. My rushed meetings with the groups to check them out allowed some students to enter the mixed groups poorly prepared to teach. Several students wrote on the course evaluations of their frustration in the mixed groups when a student from another group did not understand the material well enough to teach it. I urge you to seek advice on this situation before you begin (Johnson et al., 1991, Using Cooperative Learning; Weimer, 2002, Getting Feedback on the Climate). Prevent the problem. By contrast, when the group work goes as planned, everyone wins. Here is what a well-prepared student wrote: "Being able to contribute to the mixed groups and answer questions from the other groups really helped me to learn the material." No doubt the other students in that mixed group learned the material, too.

By the next day, day three, the students had to be prepared to teach in the mixed groups. Consider what they were undergoing. On the first day of class they were assigned two to six pages to read that day and a question to answer, and they had to type the answer. One student wrote this about the effort required for a reading assignment in the course: "Reading and understanding a paper took me from one to six hours. Writing the answer took another hour or two. On those days not much time was left for other classes." Then on the second day they handed in the answer, discussed the answer and the reading with peers to reach a consensus, and decided how they would teach it to other students. And now on the third day, they were to be assistant teachers of the course in the mixed groups, teaching members of the class whom they didn't know, and then they would synthesize all the answers into a two-page abstract of the readings that was to be typed that night for handing in the following day. They were indeed active learners.

Mixed Groups

The students were nervous on that third day. Why shouldn't they be? They were leaving their groups to join the mixed groups that consisted of a member from each group. Even though I had given them a handout with a few tips on teaching, such as keep your goal in mind (please ignore the personal irony), you have time to make one major point, arrange your ideas in sequence, nevertheless, the students were anxious. I recommended the order of presentations in the mixed groups, owing to the nature of the question each group had answered. That is, one group's answer would follow logically from another group's answer. And so they began, and I strolled around the room, pausing to listen to the presentations.

I noticed a behavior that bothered me. It was a holdover from the lecture format. Because the students were so well trained as passive note-takers for lectures, they tended to write down everything the student said who was "lecturing," with no reflection. By that I mean, a member from Group B might hear a speaker from Group A give a different interpretation from that in the Group B reading and merely note it down without comment and then, when reporting for Group B, give the other interpretation, which no one would question. That was typical passive note-taking from a lecture class. The habit was deeply ingrained and would require effort on my part to break. The mixed groups needed to have time to think about the information they were listening to, to discuss it and integrate it into a rough synthesis. But, of course, that would take even more class time. I wanted to stir this stew of information in each mixed group, but I knew the stew couldn't cook indefinitely. You have to learn how to feel your way at times like this, and I was just beginning to learn.

One aspect of my description of the mixed groups that may bother you is the replacement of an experienced lecturer (of whatever talent), namely me, by an inexperienced lecturer, a student. Even the best prepared student will not have the depth of knowledge about the topic that I have. So, isn't that shortchanging the other students? My answer is supremely wishy-washy: It all depends. If my lecture is well organized and I am excited by the material and I present the information in a manner that catches the interest of the students and I am in the first 10 minutes of my lecture (Davis, 1993, Lecture Strategies; McKeachie, 2002, How to Make Lectures More Effective), then the students would get more out of my lecture than the student's talk.

For any other situation in the lecture, I would only ask: Have you ever looked at the notes that students took in your lecture class? They will range in completeness (that can be okay) and accuracy (not good!). After looking at his students' notes, a faculty member once commented, "There was an incredible difference between what I thought I had said and the points I thought I had stressed, and what the students heard or felt was important to write down" (Davis, Wood, & Wilson, 1983). Given that the students' attention can wander wildly after the first 10 minutes of a lecture (Davis, 1993, General Strategies; McKeachie, 2002, How Can Lectures Be Improved?), the situation faced by that faculty member is but one example of Brookfield's (1995) general observation that "often, we are profoundly surprised by the diversity of meanings students read into our words and actions" (pp. 33–34). So, in this instance, and if we assume that the student speaker is competent, the student might be a more effective teacher than the faculty member. In fact, there is some evidence suggesting that

> students are able to explain concepts to one another
> more effectively than are their teachers [because] stu-
> dents who understand the concept when the question is
> posed have only recently mastered the idea and are still
> aware of the difficulties involved in grasping the con-
> cept. (Mazur, 1997, p. 13)

I think the main point, however, is that the student speaking in the mixed group is not so much a lecturer as a tutor. Research on peer tutoring concludes that although the student or group of students being tutored learn from the process of tutoring, the student tutor learns more (McKeachie, 2002, Peer Tutoring), which is a research basis to the adage that shoved me, arms flailing, into the teaching profession years before: "You never learn something until you have to teach it." Each student in the mixed group is a tutor and should learn that part of the material better than the other students; the other students, however, should learn something.

The last requirement for the mixed groups was for each mixed group to prepare a list of the main points from all the readings and answers as a synthesis of the topic. Each mixed group would then present the results of its synthesis to the whole class, and I would jot down the points on the blackboard. As a whole class, we would discuss the similarities and differences reached by the mixed groups. Finally, I would summarize the results or fill in other information as appropriate so that they learned what I had expected them to learn and had not left out anything. That was the plan, and a good plan it was. But as the class time flew by, the mixed groups remained in their tutoring stage. I think my concern with the amount of time it was taking—I had thought it would take one class period for all this activity—kept me from recognizing the inadequacy of some of the tutors. When the class period came to an end, the mixed groups had rushed into their synthesis. Now you can better appreciate why I could not have prepared the course outline in Table 5.1 before teaching the course. I simply could not estimate the time any activity would require.

On day four, the mixed groups finished their syntheses. I wrote their main points on the blackboard, and we discussed the results. Although the process went smoothly, I would have benefited from knowing better how to bring the discussion to a close in a manner that would assure me the students had learned what I expected them to learn (Davis, 1993, Bringing Closure to a Discussion; Johnson et al., 1991, Formal Cooperative Learning). "The best teachers ask concluding questions" (Bain, 2004, p. 133). Closing a lecture properly is equally important (Davis, 1993, Closing a Lecture).

I wish I could say I was happy with the way the course was going, but the old habit of "covering the material" still fought my novice plans and greatly alarmed me. Here we were in the fourth day of the course and we were not yet through the material I had covered on the second day when lecturing. I'm afraid it was here that I caught the dreaded "falling behind" disease. (And I was to fall farther behind.) So, prepare yourself from the beginning that you are not going to cover as much material as you did by lecturing, and that this condition will set off a tremendous internal tension the first time you use most types of active learning.

I'm sorry to say it, but not long after this I panicked. In order to save time and thus be able to cover more material, I did not accord this critical synthesis activity the attention it deserved. I tried to make up time, and in so doing I compromised the very purpose of the course. This is the kind of poor decision that a novice, an unskilled practitioner, can make. Thank goodness mistakes such as this can be corrected through practice, but that didn't help these students, and I'm sorry for that. My deficiencies unsettled some of my students, as you might imagine. One student expressed it this way: "Often I felt that my learning was superficial and it would ease my anxiety to hear what you view as the main points."

The cure for the falling-behind disease is obvious, though daring: Cut the amount of content to that necessary for what we want the students to learn. I know, I know—the mere mention of cutting some content raises our collective hackles as faculty because we have long habit of teaching that places "learning about" content as ... ...ue students should take from our courses. Hence, we assume that the greater the amount of content we transmit to them, the greater the value we provide them. But let's pause in my story for a moment and examine this habit that we naively embraced without question, without examination, without evaluation when first we were thrown into the classroom to sink or teach.

Two seminal reports in the initial stage of the reform of undergraduate education in science, mathematics, and engineering used research in cognitive science and pedagogy as the basis for their recommendations to reduce the content in courses. A committee of the National Research Council (1996a) concluded, "With the explosion of knowledge in all disciplines, equating quality with the coverage of as much material as possible is fundamentally misguided" (p. 22). And a committee of the National Science Foundation (1996) advised that

> the problem with a major emphasis on "covering the material" is that many of the facts that constitute this material appear to most students as nuggets of information that are both disconnected from themselves and from a context that has meaning and interest to students . . . (p. 44)

Nor is this problem restricted to science, mathematics, and engineering. Leaders in teaching in higher education who come from various disciplines have cautioned us against excess content. Parker Palmer (1998) urges us to follow William Blake's advice "to see a World in a Grain of Sand":

> Every academic discipline has such "grains of sand" through which its world can be seen. So why do we keep dumping truckloads of sand on our students, blinding them to the whole, instead of lifting up a grain so they can learn to see for themselves? Why do we keep trying to cover the field when we can honor the stuff of the discipline more profoundly by teaching less of it at a deeper level? (p. 122)

Kenneth Eble (1988) from English reprehends "the mechanical ticking off of necessary topics that constitutes 'covering' the material," because "coverage deceives the teacher about learning as much as it aids simple organization," and he concludes, "No good teacher ever included everything that should have gone into the course; wisdom is in part learning what to leave out" (p. 73). This last point is echoed by Joseph Lowman (1995) from psychology: "Because the initial list of topics is almost sure to be longer than what can be accommodated, you will have to eliminate some" (p. 201).

If I compare the textbook I used as a student in freshman physics with the textbook my students were using in freshman physics before I retired, the difference in amount of content is staggering. The pages in my textbook for a year of classes would cover a wall from floor to ceiling of a room with an eight-foot ceiling for a distance of almost 40 feet—40 feet, from floor to eight-foot ceiling. The pages of my students' textbook for a year of classes, if placed in that same room, would cover a wall from floor to ceiling for more than 80 feet. That's 80 feet. Twice as far! The students of today are not learning twice the amount of content that I learned as a student years ago. Some content that could be included today obviously is simply not included.

Suggestions for making eliminations are offered by Davis (1993, Defining and Limiting Course Content) and Prégent (1990/1994, Course Content). The point here is that we already teach less than the total amount of content in every course we teach, except for the most advanced graduate courses where the amount known from current research is very little. Therefore, to reduce the content is merely to do more of what we already do in the classroom, anyway. It is not an aberration. Nevertheless, we should be aware that if our students have to buy a textbook of 30 chapters, expecting to be assigned all the chapters to read, and instead are assigned only some chapters, with other chapters designated for background as needed and with yet other chapters completely ignored, they may well feel overcharged in money and shortchanged in content, an attitude that can resist the change in teaching.

It has been said that faculty who use active learning "have, in fact, begun to redefine 'content' to include skills and understanding, as well as information (facts, formulas, terms, names, dates, and so on)" (Meyers & Jones, 1993, p. 34). I think you can see the basis for this statement in the description of my class so far. But one of the prime justifications for emphasizing student learning over covering content is evident to those of us who teach more than one course in the department's curriculum. (It is not evident to faculty who teach but a single course in the curriculum.) Meyers and Jones put it this way: "We know that unless students actually use and appropriate ideas and information, they will not retain them much beyond the conclusion of our courses" (p. 34). Maryellen Weimer (2002) makes a stronger statement of what we have experienced:

> That students retain little understanding of course content has been documented so many times and in so many different contexts that it is impossible to list all the research—not that we need research evidence. We see it all too clearly when we teach the next course in the sequence. Sitting before us are the students who received A's and B's in the prerequisite course, and yet when asked a question that draws on prior knowledge, they look perplexed and confused; most do not venture even a guess. (p. 48)

All I knew at this time in my story was that the old habit had me in its vise. I was falling behind in covering as much content as possible. To my good fortune, I would soon discover how to limit the content covered in my course to what I thought was significant for the students to learn.

At the next class meeting, day five, the students handed in their two-page syntheses of the readings on the first topic. I could have graded them but didn't, because I didn't want the students to write for a grade. I wanted them to write in order to communicate their knowledge to me, now that they had finished the topic. Little did I know that I was trying to supplement the usual "extrinsic motivation" of students by grades with "intrinsic motivation" by their interest in the knowledge (Davis, 1993, De-emphasizing Grades; McKeachie, 2002, Intrinsic and Extrinsic Motivation). Nor did I know that the "best college teachers" studied by Bain (2004) "tried to avoid extrinsic motivators and to foster intrinsic ones" (p. 35).

I made constructive comments on the papers, particularly to point out errors, confusion, and omissions, and returned them at the next class meeting. The prompt feedback encouraged the students to check their papers with their notes and to seek further clarification with their group members, their mixed-group members, or me. Four students later wrote an article on their experience in the course for an education journal in the discipline. About the lack of grading on the syntheses, or summaries, they wrote, "The summaries were not graded; rather, the emphasis placed on the summaries was the ability to express scientific concepts. This encouraged creativity of written thought" (Housel, Huston, Martin, & Pierce, 1995, p. 331).

The next step was for the students to do something with their knowledge of the first topic. Therefore, in this class period they would work qualitative problems based on the information they had learned. The questions they would answer were of the following type: Why would you use a certain analytical method under the given conditions? Why is a variable almost constant under both normal and extreme conditions for the one situation but not for the other? Which factor limits growth in this condition, why is it the limiting factor, and how does it limit growth? Each group had a different problem to solve. The students spent the class period solving the problem as a group, thereby allowing them to gain insight to the solution by pooling the insight of all members of the group.

If you are accustomed to having each student do his or her own work, you may be put off by this arrangement. However, the effectiveness of students learning from one another is supported by research (McKeachie, 2002, Peer Learning and Teaching). In a classic study of undergraduate students, Astin (1993) reports, "Classroom research has consistently shown that cooperative-learning approaches produce outcomes that are superior to those obtained through traditional competitive approaches..." (p. 427). (See also Millis & Cottell, 1998, The Research Base.) Even in physics, a tutorial session in which groups of three or four undergraduate students, working together, solved qualitative problems following the introductory physics lecture considerably improved the students' ability to apply what they had learned in lecture (McDermott, Shaffer, & the Physics Education Group at the University of Washington, 1998).

In addition to solving their problem, my students had to prepare a presentation to explain how they had solved the problem. This arrangement shifted the emphasis from concentrating on "what is the solution?" to contemplating "how did I obtain the solution?" Now they had to think about what they had done in order to get the answer, express their thinking in their own words, and defend their reasoning, if necessary. They were articulating their problem-solving skills (Davis, 1993, Ask Students to Describe How They Solved One of Their Homework Problems; Weimer, 2002, The Function of Content). As Millis and Cottell (1998) observe: "Small groups offer an opportunity for students to explain, justify, and elaborate on their rationale for reaching conclusions" (p. 94).

Solving the problem took the entire class period. At the next class period two members of the group stayed at their station with their material while the other members of that group visited each of the other groups, picked up a copy of those problems, and listened to two members of each group explain how their problem was solved. Later, the students who had explained rotated with those who had been listening to the explanations. All in all, it took three days for this activity, and that threw me even further behind. I simply could not allot that much time to that activity; I had to change it.

Therefore, for the next year, I adjusted the structure to save a day, as shown earlier in Table 5.1. Days five and six in this table are not the activities of the first year but the activities of the second year. Rather than having each group solve a different problem, as in the first year, I gave some groups the same problem to solve by one method and other groups a different problem to solve by a second but similar method. The next day the groups paired off, taught each other how to solve their problem, turned in the solution of their problem, and received the reading for the second topic, which was to be discussed by the groups on the following day.

After another round of group discussions and mixed-group teaching of the information for the second topic, I assigned the first project. To complete the project the students had to use the knowledge they had gained from the readings, discussions, and problem solving for topics one and two. Because the course grades were based only on the projects, I'll save the discussion of the projects for the next chapter.

Reflective Questions

- *Which teaching changes (for concepts, methods, or applications) mentioned in this chapter can you list from memory?*

- *What is it about each of the teaching changes you list that makes it memorable for you?*

- *What would you want to know or need to do in order to prepare yourself to use each of these changes in your classroom?*

- *What resources are available to you to learn what you want to know or to enable you to do what you need to do in order to prepare yourself to use these changes?*

- *How would you prioritize these changes?*

- *For the teaching changes that did not appeal to you, what is the reason for the lack of appeal of each one?*

- *How might you reconsider those reasons?*

- *Why is each topic you cover in your course included for the students to learn?*

7

CHANGE MUST BE ASSESSED
FOR STUDENT LEARNING

What Is Assessment?

"Assessment" of students' learning was a vague term and concept to me when I began using cooperative learning. To many faculty it remains a vague synonym for "testing" or "evaluation," an activity that is performed by examinations at the end of the course and once or twice during the course and through weekly homework assignments—commonly graded by a graduate student and never seen by the instructor, as I well know. And, yes, that is part of it, the part that tells us how well the students *did* (past tense). But there is more to it than that. Assessment also includes finding out whether the students are "getting it" while there is still time to be flexible and make changes in our teaching to ensure that they *do* (present tense) get it before we move on to the next topic. Think of assessment as "the systematic basis for making inferences about the learning and development of students" (Erwin, 1991, p. 15). Assessment is a very complex field, particularly in conjunction with the improved understanding of human learning (National Research Council [NRC], 2001).

The first question, of course, is, What are we going to assess in our classroom?—the answer to which, since it can seem such a simple-minded question, we might toss off as, Whether they learned the material, stupid. We always have content on our mind, the subject matter of our discipline, and we do want them to learn some content and some of the skills used in our discipline. Before we look further into the learning assessment, however, I think we might benefit from a touch of modesty.

Closely related to the assessment of learning is the assessment of student development; that is, of "the ways in which people express their mode of thinking and feeling" (Erwin, 1991, p. 39)—for example, their higher-order thinking skills and personal development as a student and human being. Our touch of modesty about our subject matter content is delivered by surveys of students and alumni in which it is the developmental aspects of their education that they predict, as students, or report, as alumni, to be most important in their life after college (Erwin, 1991; Office of Educational Assessment, 1999–2003).

In the Office of Educational Assessment surveys at the University of Washington, for example, only the new freshmen and new transfer students predicted that using the knowledge, ideas, and perspectives in their discipline would be more important than defining and solving problems, locating information needed for decision-making and problem solving, and other expressions of thinking and feeling. The seniors and alumni— one, five, and ten years past graduation—assigned to the information from the major an ever decreasing importance.

Probably when you took the Teaching Goals Inventory recommended in Chapter 2, you had many goals clustered under "Discipline-Specific Knowledge and Skills." Sad to say, it's that knowledge and those skills, which you taught them, that advanced students and alums progressively mark down in importance. Holding high importance from freshmen through 10-year alums are goals of the inventory that cluster under "Higher-Order Thinking Skills," "Basic Academic Success Skills," and "Work and Career Preparation." Bain (2004) reports that many of the "best college teachers" both teach their discipline and strive to develop such intellectual habits as are dealt with in those three clusters. Therefore, the more we can enhance the students' cognitive and personal development, as well as help them learn content, the better education we provide them.

Before we can assess our students' learning, we have to know what we want the students to learn and we have to express it in such a way that we can determine whether the students are learning it (Angelo & Cross, 1993, Classroom Assessment Assumption 2; Erwin, 1991, Characteristics of Successful Assessment Programs; Fink, 2003, Appendix A: Planning Your Course: A Decision Guide; McKeachie, 2002, Planning Methods of Testing and Assessment).

By now, you are well aware of the difficulty that I had in expressing my goals for the course, an experience that the references just cited declare to be very common for faculty. (I took some comfort in learning that the shortcoming was not mine alone.) You may recall how often, when writing about my vague expectations for the students, I would say I wanted them "to know about" some topic. That is a favorite expression of faculty. But what in the world does it mean? To know about? If students memorized a single fact, wouldn't they "know about" the topic? If they memorized their lecture notes, wouldn't they "know about" the topic? Is that what we mean by "learning"? And how does one assess "to know about"? To be fair, though, I must include McKeachie's (2002) comment that "many effective teachers never state their goals very explicitly" (p. 12). Nevertheless, by the end of the term, something happened that validated for me the comforting truth of his additional comment, "Goals emerge as you teach" (p. 12). It happened like this.

Setting My Goals

Proceeding through the term at the rate that the students were learning, rather than at the rate I could lecture, we reached the end of the term and had covered only 40% of the topics I had covered by lecturing. Yes, 40%. (You thought something like that was going to happen, didn't you?) I could see it coming and had no option but to resign myself to it. Nevertheless, I felt guilty, very guilty. I felt I had shortchanged the students, deprived them of knowledge. (Please don't underestimate the guilt trip you can take from cutting the content. Habits are not easily broken. As Palmer [1998] notes, "En route to a new pedagogy, there will be days when we serve our students poorly, days when our guilt only deepens" [p. 132].)

Such a reduction in content may be simply unacceptable to you, for our habit of teaching has, as noted in the previous chapter, emphasized the amount of information covered, like the amount of food set on a table. But do students really need to be so gorged with information? My seniors had a diet meal of information, but they began to read at a graduate level, from the same textbook used in a graduate course—fewer topics but greater depth in each topic. (Less food, better nutrition!)

Contemplating the reduced coverage, however, brought me to my first understanding of my students and my expectations for them—my goals, if you will—a veritable milestone for me.

The topics I didn't cover were, naturally, the ones in the latter half of the course. But that was elimination by happenstance. The selection of topics to be included should be rational. Those topics should be—and here was a new idea for me—topics that my students could avail themselves of. That is, the knowledge the students derived from the course should have some meaning for them, both now and in the future.

Finally, I began to ask myself reflective questions about my students (Brookfield, 1995). So, how would they use the knowledge? That question led me to ask, Who were they? Oceanography majors, to be sure, but they were following four different curriculum tracks: biological oceanography, chemical oceanography, marine geology and geophysics, and physical oceanography. And 60% of them were biological oceanographers, a percentage that had held fairly constant over the years. Another percentage that had held constant was the 80% of students who did not go to graduate school, at least right away. Furthermore, almost all the students wanted to stay in the Puget Sound region for their careers. And finally, they all loved the water—they were oceanographers, after all. At last, I was on course to gain an understanding of my students (Bain, 2004; Nilson, 2003).

Therefore, the next question was, Which concepts and methods would be of use to most of the students, given the following: that my course was the only marine geology course most of them would ever take; that most would soon begin a career that, they hoped, would be in this region; and that they loved the water, which they would most likely enjoy along the shore? The answer seemed to be that they should understand, as a novice, the processes that alter the shoreline and the response of the shoreline to those processes. In addition, they should know of a major research effort in marine geology, appreciate its significance to understanding the processes and natural history of the ocean, and apprehend the methods by which it is conducted. In this way, they would both understand the happenings at the site of their main interaction with the ocean, which should have the value (Bain, 2004; Brown & Duguid, 2000) of interesting them naturally, and have one example of the kind of research marine geologists do and an informed opinion of why it was done. (I assumed that the small minority of students who were interested in continuing in marine geology would learn how to learn the discipline in my course.)

Expressing these goals was a huge step for me. By using them to form the framework of the course syllabus for the following year, I shed much of my guilt from reducing the coverage of topics, because now I knew why each topic and skill was included in the course. (This is the kind of information that you should place in your teaching portfolio [Davis, 1993, Teaching Dossier; Seldin, 2004].)

You will notice that I was still thinking in terms of topics. The next step, which came much later, was to think beyond topics, to think at last of what I wanted the students to take away from this course. I came to realize that I wanted the students to be able to walk along a beach, in fact, a shoreline, whether beach or cliff, and 1) observe the pattern of natural physical features forming the shoreline, 2) observe the strength and frequency of the processes actively affecting the shoreline features at the time of observation, 3) infer the qualitative effect of the active processes on the observed features, 4) predict changes in the features as a result of the observed strength and frequency of the processes, 5) predict changes in the features as a result of major changes in the processes that formed the features, and 6) communicate those predictions intelligibly to a lay person. Today it all seems so obvious. Why did it take me so long?

What the students needed to know first, then, was how to observe. We tend, from our lecture habit of teaching, to tell them what to look for: Look at "this," which we call a "whatchamacallit" and which signifies "such and such." But now we need to turn the procedure around and ask them "intriguing questions" (Bain, 2004, p. 100): What do you see? How might what you see be important to the future of anyone who lives here? What clues can you find that might suggest how it was formed? Is it being formed now? With their need to know, we can now tell them the name we use for the feature.

Next we can guide them to assumptions about a shoreline physical feature and ask questions about processes—what characteristics would they expect the processes that formed the feature to have? In this manner, we introduce them to the inverse reasoning that Earth scientists commonly use. And we guide them to the part of the process that formed the feature, not as a topic, not covering everything about the process that we think they should ever know, but only the part of the process that formed the feature they observed. Then we move on to the next feature they observed and repeat the procedure, and so on until all the features appropriate to their level of knowledge are discussed, not all the features we, as experts, can detect on the shoreline. Now we try to lead them to see the big picture, the underlying concept. And then we take them to another shoreline to determine whether they can apply what they have learned to a new situation and can understand what is happening, has happened, and is likely to happen there. Do they really understand the underlying concept? (I have used an example from my discipline. You might want to reread this paragraph and the preceding paragraph, replacing "shoreline" with "place," a general term with a different connotation for each discipline and therefore perhaps a more useful example for you.)

Even if your course does not have the practical application of mine, you can still use this approach. For instance, if your course is theoretical, you might follow that "intriguing question or problem" (Bain, 2004, p. 100) with basic questions about premises, assumptions, statements, and the like, and the implications of the students' answers to those questions. The point is to think, not in terms of topics of content, but in terms of the knowledge and ability to transfer that knowledge that you want the students to leave your course with. As I said, thoughts such as these came to me much later. At this point in my story, however, I had at last taken the first difficult step of setting goals for my course that I could assess.

Now, you may remark, "That's all right for you to say, but my course is a prerequisite for another course (or an accrediting examination). I have to cover all the material required for the next course (or the exam). I can't cut the content." And, yes, you are indeed in a pickle, because forces beyond your control have decided that it is more important for you to cover content than it is for the students to learn the facts, concepts, procedures, or algorithms. As Weimer (2002, How Much Content Is Enough?), observes, your decision about cutting content in a prerequisite course and using the released time to enhance the students' learning of what you think is critically important for them to learn in your course "is still a political one" (p. 67). I join her in urging caution, particularly if you are not yet tenured. Nevertheless, you might discuss with the instructor of the next course what specific prerequisite knowledge from your course is used in that course and how it is used. Guiding that instructor to reflect critically on specifics might enable you to cut some content that is not used in the next course after all. But be diplomatic. Faculty do not embrace a change that we feel lessens the "rigor" of our course and "covering a lot of content" is commonly our definition of "rigor."

Students Can Assess Their Learning and Development

Assessment of student learning can be carried out by the students or the instructor (Millis & Cottell, 1998, Part Four; Suskie, 2004; Weimer, 2002, The Purpose and Process of Evaluation). The important point for us instructors is to become aware of the various methods available for our use. The staff at your teaching center can help you with this, as can the references cited here. To ask the students to assess themselves is a new experience for most faculty, I believe. We hold doubts about the significance of the results. But the results can be revealing. For instance, one day early in the course a student left his group and came to me. He said he had always assumed that he recognized the principal ideas in whatever he read, but the discussions in his group had surprised him, for they revealed that he had overlooked some points in the readings. He thanked me for using cooperative learning. Here was successful self-assessment by a young man who was sufficiently mature to accept the results.

A simple self-assessment method is for students to compare the expressions of their learning over time. As you will find, there are several methods by which students can do this. Here is an example: On the first day of class the following year, I asked the students to take five minutes and answer the following question: How are beaches formed, maintained, and destroyed? I was ready for their blank expressions and could smile and tell them that I knew we had not studied beaches yet. (Some facial expressions clearly replied, So why are you asking us this?) Nevertheless, I wanted to know what they thought the answer to the question was. The paper they handed in would not be graded. I would ask them the same question later in the term.

Several weeks later I did ask them the same question, gave them five minutes to answer it, and collected the papers. That evening I read each student's two papers and the next day (rapid feedback) announced I was returning both papers. Without staring, I observed each student's response as I returned the first paper and then the second paper. Most did not deign to look at their first paper. They knew they had learned a great deal since that first day.

Had I been better prepared I could have told the students to make a portfolio of their returned papers and project reports, somewhat similar to a teaching portfolio. Later in the course, I could have asked them to select one of their one-page or two-page papers as evidence of their understanding of a concept or skill. Or they could have compared their first two-page paper with a later two-page paper and described how their understanding had improved. Or they could have explained in a short paper or orally how one of the project reports was evidence of their understanding.

I also read self-assessment into responses to some of the projects. The students worked on five projects, beginning with a simple one and continuing to a very complex one. The projects were designed so that the students could apply the knowledge gained from their reading, discussions, and problem solving. Knowing that the projects would have to be completed outside of class and knowing that not only was this a commuter university but that most of the students had jobs, I designed projects that required only a minimum group effort and could be completed by the individual student. This arrangement was more convenient for the students. It also benefited me by allowing me to grade each student's paper rather than a group paper. Although this arrangement is contrary to the principle of group work, it was an easy way for me to start using projects, and it eliminated the problem of assigning a grade for group work (Weimer, 2002, Group Work and Peer Assessment). True group work for grades can always be developed in following years.

For the first project, the students went to the web any time during a five-day period and viewed a regularly updated map of the areal distribution of a variable predicted from data that were taken continually from a remote sensor. They were to print out a map of the distribution from the web at that time and explain the pattern of the distribution in plain English to a lay reader. (They were required to write several of the projects in non-technical language because that prevented them from using technical terms as a fog to conceal a lack of understanding. We instructors tend to read a misstatement of a technical term and think, Well, that's not exactly right but I know what he means. But, in truth, we may not know what he means.)

The simple objectives of the project were for the students to observe data, describe the pattern produced by the data, and explain it with their knowledge of the process producing it. It so happened that the computer most students used was in a room next to my office. One day I happened to overhear a conversation that I have treasured ever since. A student walked into the computer room, greeted another student, and said, "Man, that pattern looks nothing like what I got yesterday." He apparently pulled out his map and the two students proceeded to discuss what the differences in the two patterns at different times meant. And they knew what they were talking about. To me they were expressing self-assessment of their learning. I leaned back in my desk chair with a limitless smile, punched my fists at the ceiling, and hissed to myself, "Yes-s-s-s-s!" They had learned it. I was doing something right. Oh, the joy of it! The pure joy!

The project that best assessed the difference in the students' development between my lecture class and the cooperative learning class was one that had been a homework problem in lecture. The students were given a letter written by a fictitious couple who had read an article in the newspaper, like the one attached to the letter, about natural hazards along the shoreline. They had also read in a book on shoreline hazard assessment in Puget Sound that their property had a certain hazard assessment. They were asking the students to examine their property and write them a short report on whether the students agreed with the book's assessment or not and give the reasons for their decision. I let each student "locate" the property wherever he or she wished it to be on the shores of Puget Sound. The students had already discussed the general nature of the Puget Sound shoreline and had examined atlases of the shoreline.

Back when I lectured, I had always hoped that the students would respond to my question about their results on the day they handed in their report. I would ask them to say something about what they had found. Of course, you know what happened, year after year. Silence! A long silence before my begging would persuade someone to speak, for maybe half a minute, and always he or she would remain seated. Now I was standing in the cooperative learning classroom, hugging their reports to my chest. The time had come. I squeezed the papers harder against me and, once more gathering up confidence out of nothing, asked the ancient impotent question: Who will be the first to tell us what you found?

Before I could even hold my breath in eager hope, two or three students shot up their hands. I managed to find voice and call on one of them. She got up, and she went to the blackboard, and she began sketching the site of her study. I was delighted. She spoke briefly and persuasively of her conclusion. I was doubly delighted. She was applauded. I was giddy. And around the room we went. Every student went to the board, spoke impromptu, and two students even exchanged a low-five as the speaker returned to her seat. I didn't want that class ever to end, but it did, and the students trickled out in lighthearted conversation. I floated joyously back to my office. Years later I happened upon this line by Hebert and Loy (2002), caught my breath, and hoped it had also applied to that day in class: "On the days when everything clicks, there is an almost magical feeling present in students and teachers, which remains for a lifetime; these are moments of true mastery" (p. 205).

I confess that I cannot tell you that the subject matter content in those papers was significantly better than that in the papers of the lecture classes. There were too many different sites, just too many variables, and the grading of reports like those is very subjective. The average grade of the papers from this class was about the same as that from the lecture class the year before. That said, there is no doubt in my mind that the students' development in thinking, attitude, and communication during their group work had given them a confidence and capability that was lacking in the lecture students. And that was personal development, and that was what the surveys of students and alumni reported to be held in greater value after graduation. And that was wonderful indeed to behold.

Not all self-assessment of projects brought me such joy. After I had returned the papers for another project, one of the brightest students in the class casually told me, "We didn't learn anything in this project that we hadn't learned doing the previous one." My first response was, "Why is this student talking to me like this?" But when I examined the two projects, I realized that by recycling an old homework problem as a project because I was in a bind for time, I had done what she said. I replaced the project the next year. Once more in partnership with a student I was able to improve the course. Whereas once upon a time I had ignored students' comments of all kinds, now I treasured them.

In addition to self-assessment, they had one opportunity for peer assessment (Millis & Cottell, 1998, Peer Assessment). However, I didn't go all the way with this assessment, because they were assessing the results of a project, which was for a grade, and I was not sufficiently prepared to defend having part of their grade be the responsibility of their peers. It was a project in which the students made posters targeted at a lay audience. This project was completed in class as group work. Their grade was not based on their poster, however. I gave them guidelines for reviewing posters to recommend improvements, in the manner that a colleague might review a draft of a poster before a researcher made the final copy to present at a meeting. For their grade, Group 1 reviewed the poster by Group 2, Group 2 reviewed that by Group 3, and so forth.

In this sense, it was a peer assessment and the students reviewed as a group. However, each student wrote his or her own report, which eliminated any group grade, and I graded them on the basis of their adherence to the guidelines for reviewing posters, which eliminated a peer determination of anyone's grade. Coming up with a consistently fair grading method for this project, after the fact, was a real headache. I think McKeachie's (2002) comment about exams also applies to projects: "[Those] that are the easiest to construct are the most difficult to grade and vice versa" (p. 75).

There were a couple of separate learning moments with respect to the posters, one of which slipped by me. The instructor of the evening introductory oceanography course consented to let his students review the posters and rank them for "successful presentation of content in an attractive and understandable manner." These reviewers thus approximated a lay audience. When I gave the reviews to my students, we had a learning moment. I heard several students explode in exasperation over the complaint that most of the posters were too technical. To an accompaniment of nodding heads and muttered "That's right," one student declared, "What's wrong with those guys? We've already dumbed it down."

I could be cynical and predict that the students were already learning to be professors, but in truth, they had learned how difficult it is to communicate the subject matter of their discipline to a lay audience. Here was a learning moment that I let get away from me, for that was a time "when something unexpected but important happens in class and your agenda must be scrapped" (Palmer, 1998, p. 146). I should have seized the opportunity to open a discussion about what would improve communication between scientists and the public, a very important subject. Alas, I clung to my agenda and the moment came and passed without my recognizing it—until it was too late.

Instructors Can Assess Student Learning

Of course, we instructors do most of the assessing, usually through the use of grades. This kind of assessment is a summation: To what level did each student measure up? There is usually precious little we can do for those who don't measure up very high because, our constructive comments on the papers aside, we have moved on to another topic before we even return the graded papers. There is another type of assessment, though, which we seldom use and which I'll discuss in a moment, but for now let me tell you about the graded assessment in my course.

As you know, I gave no exams in the course—and was glad to be rid of them. So were the students. One student wrote, "The absence of testing was wonderfully liberating." Several students wrote that exams were for "simply regurgitating memorized material" and "cramming for midterms and finals—only to forget the material the next day." I had always had trouble creating good exams, a fault that probably resulted from my poor knowledge of what examination is all about (Davis, 1993, Quizzes, Tests, and Exams; McKeachie, 2002, Assessing, Testing, and Evaluating). You, however, may want to give exams, even group exams (Millis & Cottell, 1998, Group Grading; Weimer, 2002, Role of the Teacher, Principle 5).

Early in the course I began taking novice steps at changing the way I graded from docking one point here, two points there, and so forth to establishing a crude scoring rubric, without knowing what a rubric was. That is, I was establishing criteria for the components of the project report that I expected the students' work to satisfy. The idea was to grade the students, not one against the others, but all against a standard of what I expected. It made little sense to create a cooperative learning environment and then turn around and grade the students competitively against one another. To be honest, I didn't travel very far down that road, only a few steps toward establishing a standard (Walvoord & Anderson, 1998, Establishing Criteria and Standards for Grading).

By the second year I had a better grasp of what I was trying to do, although I was still learning. For instance, the handout I gave the students for a project included the grading scale. The highest score required the use of references other than the textbook, the explanation integrated the problem with other processes, the information was presented not only clearly and accurately but creatively and professionally, and the illustrations were sufficient for understanding critical aspects. The next level below required the use of only the textbook, the explanation referred descriptively to other processes, the information was presented clearly and accurately, and only a single generalized illustration was included. It takes time to change all parts of a course from lecture to cooperative learning or other forms of active learning. I urge you to be patient.

You may wonder how the course grades by cooperative learning and projects compared with those by lecture and examination. I find it difficult to draw much of a conclusion about the average grades, because of the different basis for grading examinations and projects. The average grades for the cooperative learning class are slightly higher, not because more students made 4.0s, but because fewer students made low grades. In contrast to my ignorance of why some students made low grades in the lecture course, I knew why the few students made low grades in the cooperative learning course: they didn't understand the concepts. In fact, a couple of them didn't understand some basic science and math. That discovery saddened me, doubly so because the students were seniors.

Let me digress for a moment, in case you feel shortchanged in my seemingly offhand comparison of student achievement in cooperative learning with that in conventional lecture. As mentioned in Chapter 6, the effectiveness of students learning from one another has been well documented (see Astin [1993] and the references in Millis & Cottell [1998, The Research Base] and in NRC [2000, Research on Inquiry-Based Science Teaching]). As for achievement in cooperative learning in particular, Johnson, Johnson, and Stanne's (2000) large meta-analysis concluded that the various methods of cooperative learning, if implemented effectively, promoted higher achievement than conventional competitive or individual learning, as determined by tests, grades, quality of reports, and so forth.

Here are three analyses as specific examples of the effectiveness of various formats of active learning, including cooperative learning, over conventional teaching by lecture. The active learning students were found to 1) earn "more quality grades (A, B, C) than their counterparts" in several undergraduate chemistry courses (Peer-Led Team Learning, 2004, Comparing the Performance . . .); 2) "outperform the control group on conceptual problems in chemistry and on scientific thinking problems" (ChemConnections, n.d., Comparative Design Studies); 3) "improve student retention, produce no decrease in content knowledge, promote deeper understanding of course material, and increase logical thinking skills" in an introductory geology course (McConnell, Steer, & Owens, 2003, p. 205); and 4) exhibit an improved overall performance in geography (Gibbs, Haigh, & Lucas, 1996, p. 181). So that I don't mislead you into thinking enhancement of learning through active learning is a given, the NRC (2000) cautions us that improvements can be modest in some cases, and Johnson et al. (2000, Discussion) caution that positive results are not guaranteed.

The projects and their grades in my course were the summation form of assessing the students' learning and development—summative assessment; the other type of assessment that faculty can conduct checks the students' learning while it is still forming—formative assessment—and there is time for us to correct problems with the learning (Erwin, 1991). A treasury of these assessment techniques is found in the book by Angelo and Cross (1993), *Classroom Assessment Techniques*. These techniques can be used regardless of the teaching format, from active learning to lecture. They include such techniques as the Background Knowledge Probe to find out the levels of pertinent background knowledge the students possess before a topic is introduced, the Minute Paper to find out what the students think is the most important thing they have learned in class that day or week, the Muddiest Point to find out what points are the most difficult for the students to understand, and Concept Maps to find out how the students associate concepts. (For examples of these classroom assessment techniques applied to courses in science, mathematics, engineering, and technology, see the Field-tested Learning Assessment Guide, online at the National Institute for Science Education, n.d.).

In a cooperative learning class, however, I had the additional benefit of listening to the students' discussions and adapting the activity in the classroom to respond to their learning difficulties. These changes were responses to assessment. For instance, when the students were discussing the topic that they would present in a poster, I realized—as noted on my page for that day's class—that they did not grasp the concept of estuarine sedimentation well. (Had I been lecturing and thought to pause and ask whether there were any questions, I probably would have heard the usual silence.) The next day I gave an illustrated mini-lecture on the aspect of the subject with which they were having difficulty.

By the second year, I recognized the importance of assessing the group's effectiveness; that is, how well people in the group were working together to complete the assignment (Davis, 1993, Evaluating Group Work; Millis & Cottell, 1998, Promoting Learning Through Responsible Assessment; Stein & Hurd, 2000, Team Evaluation). I didn't touch that the first year, but the second year I asked the students for their opinion about both a self-assessment form that asked about their participation in the group and a peer-assessment form that asked about the participation of the other members of the group. It will probably not surprise you that most of the students (68%) thought the self-assessment form could be useful and that even more of them (85%) wanted nothing to do with the peer review. From the attitude represented by these votes, I realized that I had to put much more planning into the peer review, or "group processing" as it is called. This peer review is a way to resolve problems that arise in a group while they are still small. By all means, seek guidance from the literature or your teaching center on using group processing assessment in your class.

Reflective Questions

- *How well can you take what you want your students to learn in one topic/lesson/module in the course and state it in such a manner that you can assess whether they are learning it?*

- *How well can you take what you want your students to be able to do with what they learn for that topic/lesson/module and state it in such a manner that you can assess whether they are learning it?*

- *What would the students have to do to convince you that they are learning what you want them to learn and that they can use that learning?*

- *Assume you asked the students to write a three-minute answer to the question, "What was the most important thing you learned in class today?" Assume that 50%, 30%, and 10% of the students missed the point of the class. How would you respond to the results of this assessment in the situation of each percentage?*

- *What does a student's grade in your course tell you about that student as a learner?*

8

CHANGE MUST BE ASSESSED FOR TEACHING

We are informed that "learning is not necessarily an outcome of teaching" (American Association for the Advancement of Science Project 2061, 1990, p. 198). Therefore, having set our goal to enhance student learning, we should feel obliged to assess our teaching for whether we are indeed helping the students to learn better. We can choose among several methods for this assessment, the most common being the end-of-term evaluations of the course by the students, a Midterm Class Interview, and faculty peer review (Davis, 1993, Evaluation to Improve Teaching; McKeachie, 2002, How Can You Get and Use Feedback to Improve Your Teaching?).

Regardless of the assessment method suggested, this subject does not interest most faculty. We already know the reasons for this lack of interest. I have mentioned the student evaluations before and a common tendency for us to ignore them or to be hurt or angered by the complaints in them. To forgo this criticism appeals to us. And when I was lecturing, the mere thought of an outsider entering my classroom to interview my students about my teaching or a faculty peer coming to observe me while teaching would have violated my precious seclusion on the classroom island. Underlying those feelings was my conviction that there was nothing I could do to improve my teaching except change the content. This conviction is commonly held by faculty.

Now I know that I can indeed change my teaching in ways that improve the students' learning, but in order to change I need to know how I'm doing at present. And if I am using a form of active learning—in my class it's cooperative learning—I must be cognizant that an assessment of my teaching must take adaptation and flexibility into account, or else the assessment is biased against me from the start. Teaching by active learning requires an adaptability and flexibility in the instructor that is not practiced by most lecturers, but that is used by the best of them (Bain, 2004). Weimer (2002) refers to this requirement as "tinkering," and encourages us: "To have to adjust techniques before and as we use them is not a sign of incompetence. To figure out what is wrong and fix it so that it runs well for you and your students is a sign of pedagogical prowess" (p. 189).

Adaptation and Flexibility

Although discussion in groups followed by teaching in mixed groups was the basic structure of the course, had that been the only structure, the students would have become as bored with it as with a daily lecture. Part of my adaptation as instructor was to alter the structure as appropriate. Twice, instead of having the students apply their knowledge in the form of problem solving, I had them apply it as a whole class by answering questions I asked them about some feature or process shown in a 35mm slide or an overhead transparency. This arrangement also aimed at a different learning style than problem solving (Davis, 1993, Learning Styles and Preferences; McKeachie, 2002, Full Participation in Learning; Nilson, 2003, Teaching to Different Learning Styles), not that I appreciated that aspect of what I was doing.

I quickly caught on that in a cooperative learning course the need for flexibility is often unanticipated, particularly the first time the course is taught. For example, even after finding separate readings for the groups at the proper level of comprehension and with overlapping content, I had to change the reading a couple of times when we reached a topic. In one instance, I realized that the readings were going into too much detail. For another topic, the readings would have been a little too advanced for the level of understanding that the students demonstrated with the previous readings. On three occasions I determined from the sluggish and hesitant group discussions that the students were having great difficulty in understanding a topic. I obviously had not selected a set of readings from which the students were able to learn. So I gave a lecture on what I wanted them to learn. (Yes, I reverted to lecturing. It was the only solution I was prepared to use.) By so doing, however, I pushed back the schedule, which meant that some topic down the line would not be covered, or covered so thoroughly as planned. Welcome to one of those recurring self-defining decisions for the active learning teacher. In this instance, the question was, Which is more important? Covering as much of the material as possible or ensuring that the students learned the material covered? In a crisis, the answer cannot be "both."

Another adaptation was my insertion of an unplanned activity in order to prevent two writing assignments from falling due on the same day. Assigning numerous writing assignments required me to pay close attention to the day that the assignment would be due. Another time, I scrapped separate readings for each group, assigned all groups the same reading, and then led a whole-class discussion of their answers to the focus question for that reading. This change eliminated the mixed-group teaching and, by cutting two days from that topic, kept the students from having to go into mixed groups for their teaching the same day as a midterm exam in another course. By eliminating the mixed-group structure, I allowed them to spend their time studying for the exam instead of having to divide their time between that studying and preparing to teach in my course. The change was an act of partnership for me and the students, who had told me of the upcoming exam. They appreciated my adaptation. I benefited from their openness.

Let me give you a detailed description of one of these adaptations. It resulted in the posters that became the peer assessment described in Chapter 7. (From the description of the exercise in Chapter 7, I'll bet you assumed that it had been planned that way from the beginning. Guess again!) When we got to the topic of estuarine sedimentation, I realized that the one-page and two-page writing assignments would be due too soon for the students to complete them satisfactorily if I kept the jigsaw structure. By that I mean that they had just handed in a project report that had been difficult to write, owing to the complexity of the project. The study of estuarine sedimentation would not take them more than two days, with a writing assignment each day. Then they would have another project to write up. That was a lot of writing in a short time after a difficult writing assignment. The students needed a break. Consequently, I assigned all groups the same reading for discussion instead of the various readings I had selected. So, what would be the object of their discussion now that they would not be writing a one-page paper or meeting in mixed groups and writing a two-page summary?

The idea of preparing a poster came to mind. Each group would prepare a two-foot by three-foot poster on the essential information that a lay person in the Puget Sound region should know about estuarine sedimentation. Each group would design a poster; self-assign responsibilities for text, graphics, and so forth; and create the poster in class. (As I have mentioned, that my university is a commuter university rendered the assignment of group activities outside class time an imposition on the students, even though some groups did function on their own as study groups. Therefore, the posters had to be created in class. Of course, had I chosen computer posters, the posters could have been created outside class.) But the students would need time between discussing poster responsibilities (Monday) and preparing the posters (Thursday). I used Tuesday to everyone's advantage by giving the mini-lecture on the aspects of the concept that I heard them stumbling over in their discussions the day before. And on Wednesday I shamelessly showed them a video on a topic I thought they ought "to know about."

After seeing the posters they produced, which were products of considerable planning and effort, I knew that the adaptation had been valuable. I also realized that the students should be appropriately rewarded for work that greatly exceeded my expectations. Thus I came up with the idea of having the students vote for the best poster, which would be placed in a display case in the building as public recognition, and with the idea of having the students review the posters as an activity for which each student could be graded. In this manner the posters became a project with a writing assignment that differed in objectives from those for the previous projects.

Incidentally, although the outline of this mode of teaching (shown earlier in Table 5.1) appears complex and rigid, by now you should appreciate that it is in reality extremely flexible, as demonstrated by the example just given. Guest lecturers can be easily inserted. The limit is your controlled imagination. Let me give an example of the difference a year can make in the growth of one's imagination, by comparing the first and second years of my using cooperative learning.

As the course neared the end of the term, the students evinced concern over their grades. In response, I offered them a small bonus project that over half the class undertook. They were to select an aspect of a natural process that they had just read about and discussed, select a scientific problem in that aspect that interested them, and write a pre-proposal for funding to do research on that problem. I wish I could declare I knew at the time that having the students, by the end of the course, pose the questions and determine what constituted data enhanced their learning (Bransford, Brown, & Cocking, 1999) and constituted part of learning by inquiry (National Research Council [NRC], 2000), but in truth I was simply too pooped to come up with anything else for them or me to do. We were all beat, the students as well. I even made the last day of class voluntary—and still more than half the class showed up. God love 'em! They turned in some fine papers, including some with hypotheses and suggested methods for testing those hypotheses.

The second year I had better defined my goals, which included having the students learn about a major research program being conducted in this discipline so that they could appreciate the kind of research carried on by professionals in the discipline. I chose the same research program that had been the bonus project for the first year and enhanced it. In so doing, I attained Stage 6 of the stages of concern about innovation (shown earlier in Table 4.1), refocusing: "I have some ideas about something that would work even better." Here is how I used my imagination for the students to prepare for the report that year.

On Monday they met in their groups to discuss a reading on facts and the general description of the region, in other words, background facts. For Tuesday, they had read about the local system of processes, each person in the group had prepared a list of five questions that he or she thought the answers to which were most important for understanding the system, and in their groups they reached an understanding of the system as best they could.

For Wednesday, they had read about the specific process that I had selected within the local system of processes and prepared five questions about the aspect of the specific process of greatest interest to each. The class then divided into special groups based on common interest of aspect, discussed their questions, the specific process and the local system, and the background information. For Thursday, each person in the group reported on one reference found online that was pertinent to the common interest, and each group reached a consensus on the questions they would like the visitor to answer on Monday.

On Monday, three colleagues who were leaders in the research program came to class. The special groups met with the appropriate visitor for answers to their questions about the specific process. On Tuesday, the special groups met for debriefing in preparation for each person to write a project report. (To this day, the three professors who visited that class remember the quality of the questions that the students asked them.) But this was the closest I came to having the students learn by inquiry, which is the basis for the reform of science education (American Association for the Advancement of Science Project 2061, 1993; NRC, 1996a, 1996b, 2000; National Science Foundation, 1996). That could come later. Nevertheless, I was using my imagination and creativity in my classroom. I was neither bored nor boring. Your imagination and creativity can make the cooperative learning classroom an exciting place for students to learn.

Perhaps the most difficult adaptation that you will have to make is giving up complete control of the classroom. Oh, you are still in charge, all right. It's just that you are no longer isolated at the front of the room, tucked safely behind the lectern, able to ignore any raised hands that you do not want to acknowledge. You should say to yourself, "I am no longer the fount of knowledge. I am a facilitator, walking around the room, assisting when required. I am out on the floor, being asked questions from out of the blue, sometimes about topics having nothing to do with what is being studied."

A question I have often been asked by young faculty members and graduate students is how I answered questions to which I didn't know the answer. Simple: "I don't know" was my answer to many questions. If I felt I ought to know the answer, particularly in other sub-disciplines, I would try to find it. Perhaps letting students witness the limits of professorial knowledge is educational for them, but it can be embarrassing, though not so embarrassing as when the limit was revealed from behind the lectern. The informality of the cooperative learning classroom diminishes guilt of ignorance, for teacher as well as students. More generally, it reduces the risk attendant to learning. I should add that if I thought the students ought to know the answer to the question they asked me, I would answer them with a question to get them thinking about the answer to their question. A very bright student told me years later, "I hated to come to you with a question, because you always answered a question with a question and I had to think what you might ask me." That was the whole idea.

The greatest test of my imagination and flexibility—and the greatest risk of failure—was my decision to require the students to undertake a project for which they had to learn something I didn't know how to teach them. This challenge does not exist when we emphasize the information that we put into the course rather than the learning the students take out of it. The situation was another example of the kind of self-defining crisis moment you can encounter in active learning. My decision to do it informed me that I had indeed set my goal to enhance student learning rather than cover the material, in spite of my worry over falling behind. Think back to that evening course years before, in which I had simply deleted the topics that I didn't know how to teach. How much I had changed! Now I was thinking of my students rather than myself.

Here was the situation: The students had read and discussed several concepts of a particular natural process along a shore and had learned several equations that expressed those concepts. Now I wanted them to take some data, decide which concepts to apply, decide which equations to use, make some assumptions, and from their calculations estimate the rate of that process. The traditional form of an exercise like this was to hand the students a sheet of paper, or sheets of paper, of printed data. But I wanted them to be more active. I wanted them to take the data off the web. In fact, I wanted them to monitor data from a nearshore buoy for a month. The data from that buoy would be theirs, not mine, thus giving them ownership of the data.

The only catch was that at that time I did not know how to download the data, enter it in a spreadsheet, and manipulate the data in the spreadsheet. A quandary! What with everything else going on in the course, I didn't have time to learn how to do all of that. Nevertheless, I refused to resort to a handout. Even though I did not have the skills, I knew that my students should possess those skills before they graduated from the university. I also knew that the students did not use computers in other courses in their major at that time. So when I handed out the description of the project in class, I assumed as calm and confident a bearing as I could muster and, in a voice once more far steadier than my churning vitals, I asked for a show of hands of those students who knew how to download from the web into a spreadsheet. I further asked them if they would please teach the other students. They did. Thank heavens! In yet another way, students had become assistant teachers. The project was underway—to my great relief and exhilaration. But how would I know whether the answers they got were correct, since I couldn't work the problem myself?

My solution was to require the students to include in their paper an example in which they made calculations by hand as their verification that the "black box" of the computer program was doing what they expected it to do. Although the example allowed me to grade their work, it had a more serious purpose. It cautioned them to be aware of the hammer (computer program) as well as the nail (the data) as they sought their goal (Polanyi, 1962). Researchers have been known to use "black boxes" with which they are unfamiliar to produce results that may or may not be valid.

Every alteration required me to be flexible and to realize that each alteration risked failure. But I never dwelt on failure. When a student was absent I had to be prepared to take that student's place in the group or mixed group. I was particularly needed in a mixed group, for otherwise the information from one group would not be shared with the members from the other groups in that mixed group. Therefore, I reread the reading assignments for all the groups and reviewed the focus questions before each class meeting for group work. Although this may seem like a lot of work, it's no more than reviewing one's lecture notes before a day's lecture.

Keeping on my toes challenged me, for sure. It also inspired me. Nevertheless, to see a cooperative-learning instructor stroll around the classroom, pausing beside the groups, chatting with this group and that, can lead a visitor to assume that the teacher has little responsibility. Yeah, right! It goes unseen. From my description of the class, you may be able to appreciate that much of the adaptation and flexibility you will apply to your course can likewise be missed by the tools for assessing your teaching (McManus, 2001). Be that as it may, this assessment can provide you with information to help you better attain your goal of enhancing the students' education.

Assessment of Teaching by Student Evaluation

The standard end-of-term student evaluation of instructors usually comes in two forms—a set of questions or statements about the course and the instructor to be scored from 1 to 5 by the students and a few questions for short answers. As I said in Chapter 2, let's join a long list of informed faculty who ignore the standardized questions or statements. As McKeachie (2002) remarks, "The questions on the form are so general that they may be irrelevant to a particular class and, even if relevant, are worded so generally that they offer little guidance for improvement" (p. 326). Weimer (2002) adds that the questions asked "do not provide the diagnostic, descriptive details that help faculty make informed choices about what to change" (p. 196). Palmer (1998) asserts that "the nuances of teaching cannot possibly be captured this way. No uniform set of questions will apply with equal force to the many varieties in which good teaching comes" (p. 142).

At my university two of the four statements that appear on every type of evaluation form used and that are averaged for a handy-dandy numerical rating of faculty teaching are ambiguous for cooperative learning. The statements to be rated are "The instructor's contribution to the course was . . ." and "The instructor's effectiveness in teaching the subject matter was . . ." Each statement can be rated low by students who assume that an instructor who didn't lecture didn't contribute or teach. Brookfield (1995) rejects all questions but those "that would probe the extent to which students felt that they had been stretched, challenged, questioned, and introduced to alternative perspectives" (p. 253). Well-chosen short-answer questions can meet Brookfield's requirement. (See Weimer [2002] for suggestions and references. In fairness, also see Davis [1993, Student Rating Forms]; McKeachie [2002, Feedback from Students]; and Perry & Smart [1997] for benefits of student ratings.)

The four short-answer questions for my class were: 1) Did you find this class to be intellectually challenging? Yes. No. Why or why not? 2) What aspects of this class contributed most to your learning? 3) What aspects of this class detracted from your learning? 4) What suggestions do you have for improving this class? Because I wanted more information from the students than I would expect from allowing them just the last 10 minutes of the class period to answer the questions, I let them take the forms home and turn them in to the university the next day. Of the 22 students, 17 returned the forms, with far more comments than usual for a course evaluation. One student even wrote on his or her form, "I would also like to point out that I would not have been able to comment in this manner before taking this course."

When the forms came back to me after the term was over, I took the envelope out of my mailbox with conflicting emotions. Part of me hoped ever so much that the enjoyment I had drawn from the course and that I believed I had seen reflected in the students' attitudes in class was recorded in their answers. Another part of me feared the harsh comments that had always marked my evaluations. I took the envelope back to my office, placed it on my desk, and sat staring at it for a long time. My joy had vanished. Finally, I opened the envelope and took out the standardized form and the 17 yellow pages of short answers. As I scanned the answers, my joy returned—in glorious, room-filling waves of exhilaration.

Here is one positive comment from each of the 17 students' answers about their learning, as they perceived it:

- "The Format was wonderful. Students could focus on learning rather than cramming for mid-terms and finals—only to forget the material the next day."

- "The class made us think out the concepts ourselves without just spoon feeding us the answers."

- "We actually got to get involved in the learning process."

- "I believe this is a better way to learn."

- "We not only learned geology, but many other useful tools that will help me in the future in science."

- "Traditionally a student will read, listen, then take a test. Dr. McManus focused on <u>how</u> to use the information. These skills are applicable to all forms of learning."

- "Having to try and teach material <u>really</u> makes one learn, and in order not to look <u>stupid</u> we had no choice but to learn."

- "I honestly believe that I learned more under this format of teaching."

- "I feel that I did learn and that I was <u>excited</u> about the material. I would leave class and would talk about both the material and the class format to anyone who would listen."

- "The material was challenging (sometimes even difficult to understand) but being able to understand after discussion with other students was exciting."

- "I think this was the most challenging, and rewarding class I have ever taken."

- "Having to take what I learned and present it to other class members proved to be challenging, yet fun."

- "Work load was incredible (you made us do your job) but I don't know if I would change that."

- "No critique is possible because this class is the best class I have had in any college I have been to. The amount of stuff was large but that was what got me excited about learning."

- "I have learned more in this class than in the majority of other classes I have taken at the university, and I think it is largely attributable to the format and style of teaching."

- "I learned more and was able to retain more information than in any other class I've had at this school. The teaching style was by far the most constructive I have encountered."

- "Definitely continue the experiment!"

Let me repeat, these comments are the students' perceptions of their experience, and must be accepted as perceptions, not facts. Nevertheless, the number of students who perceived that they had learned in the class is remarkable and heartening. They had been challenged, and therefore I believe that their answers are of a kind that would meet Brookfield's (1995) requirement for credible student evaluations. Further, I believe that Eble (1983) is right when he says,

> Clearly, there is nothing more fundamental to learning
> than giving attention to the task. Attention registers in
> as obvious physical ways as smiles and laughter. If, in
> the end, a range of attentive responses results in stu-
> dents actually saying they were pleased, why should we
> distrust their response, fear they are conning us or
> deceiving themselves about easy pleasures as against
> hard learning? (pp. 48–49)

And what of their answers to the question what aspects of the class detracted from their learning? Here is one comment from each of 13 students; four students either stated there were no detractions or left the question blank.

- "At times the group method seemed ineffective if all the members were confused."

- "In some cases the material was not clearly understood in the small groups."

- "When I absolutely did not understand something."

- "When we broke up into mixed groups, other members often had either not prepared or just did not understand the material."

- "I feel the mixed groups should be more structured."

- "Sometimes writing all those summaries got to be a little much. I really felt stressed all of the time."

- "Sometimes there was so much reading and papers that it was hard to spend enough time on one thing to really learn it."

- "I was not detracted from learning in the class, but I felt some of my other classes were being neglected so that I could do well in this class."

- "Time constraints from outside detracted. Nothing in class detracted."

- "Sometimes 'time' was a problem. If groups got done discussing before other groups, more stuff in class could help."

- "Group work could be a social thing."

- "The detraction for me was not knowing what to expect."

- "Main points of material were sometimes vague."

These comments can be grouped by aspect. Of the 13 students who mentioned an aspect that detracted from their learning, five mentioned the lack of understanding by members of the group or mixed group. This detraction was my fault for not spending enough time with the groups to ensure that all members understood the material. This could be corrected. Four students stated that having too much work detracted from their learning, but two students felt that having too little work detracted. Two students' comments might be grouped under the heading of their not receiving explicit expectations. (By contrast, one student from this class told me several years later that one of the attractions of the class for her was that she never knew what was going to happen each day.) Here we see the diversity of student perceptions. All in all, I was satisfied with the students' perception of this change in the way I taught. The positives far outweighed the negatives, and the most serious detraction to the students' learning could be remedied, though only by major effort on my part. I could accept that—gladly.

Outsiders Can Assess Student Learning

We are so accustomed to the seclusion of our classroom—just the students and us—that the thought of someone else coming into the room is upsetting. That they would dare to assess the students' learning or our teaching can feel threatening. Yet the students can respond readily to a stranger who is trained in obtaining a Midterm Class Interview or Small

Group Instructional Diagnosis (SGID) (Center for Instructional Development and Research [CIDR], 2004b). The procedure is performed by a consultant at your teaching center and works like this. (When I was a faculty associate at CIDR, the teaching center of the University of Washington, I learned to perform this interview.)

The consultant will discuss with you whether this form of assessment is appropriate for you; for instance, a requirement is that you are open to changing the class if the students suggest a change that could improve their learning. The consultant will then ask you what you want to get out of the process and what your perspective of the course is. The two of you will agree on a day when the consultant can come to the class and have 20 minutes or so alone with the students to obtain their perspective of their learning. At that time, the students are requested to form small groups and try to reach a consensus answer, with examples, to a couple of questions, such as, "What helps you learn in this course?" and "What changes could be made in the course to assist you in learning?" Each group is handed a form on which to write their answers. After 10 minutes, the groups report out to the whole class while the consultant seeks consensus, nature of disagreement, intensity of feelings, and so forth. The consultant then takes the notes on the whole class discussion and the group forms for analysis so as to identify themes, strengths of the learning, problems with the learning, and recommendations.

At a later meeting with the consultant, you receive a report and an explanation of the information. I found that the main benefit from the process is that owing to the students being asked for their opinion, they interpreted the process to mean that you cared about their learning. Few instructors make caring explicit. The best do (Bain, 2004). And if you explain why you are unable to make certain changes they recommended and you do make some other changes they recommended, a closer relationship develops between you and the students. Lessening the distance between instructor and students always enhances learning. Another benefit is that the consultant can provide knowledge and experience on how to make changes, which is critical. If you ask the students for their opinion and thereby imply that you care about their learning, but then ignore their recommendations to improve their learning, you have poisoned the atmosphere of your class.

Other outsiders who can provide assessment of the students' learning and your teaching are your colleagues, who can provide peer assessment (Chism, 1999). However, before you consider this approach, be certain that the faculty members who will assess you and your class fully understand what you are attempting to accomplish. Otherwise, mistakes on their part can make you look terrible (Hutchings, 1996; McManus, 2001).

As you can see from this description of my experience, assessment can give you a strong sense of what is going on in your class: how well the students are learning, how effectively the students are working together in their groups, and how effective you are as a teacher. And you can take the time to make changes, if necessary, to improve the conditions for their learning. If the assessment at the end of a section of the course is based on an activity that pertains to the real world, then you also have a sense of how well the students can apply their learning to a situation more like the real world than any test is. Just don't cancel the assessments. There will be an urge to do this.

In planning my course for the second year, I included several self-assessments for the students. The question on the first day of class, repeated later in the term, I carried out. All the others I canceled, because when I reached each of those points in the term, the total assignments of readings, one-page papers, two-page synopses, project research, and project reports seemed so much that I couldn't bring myself to add another assignment, a self-assessment. It takes time for us to appreciate the value we, and the students, can obtain from these assessments of the students' learning. Don't cancel them in order to cover content.

Reflective Questions

- *List three examples of adaptation or flexibility in your daily life. What goal, mission, vision, or value allowed you to make those changes?*

- *How might you apply that ability to your course in order to enhance the students' learning?*

- *What short-answer questions on end-of-term evaluations would you like your students to answer?*

- *Under what conditions would you change your course in response to the students' answers to those questions?*

- *In what ways might the presentation in this book help you make those changes more easily?*

- *What questions come to mind with respect to requesting a Midterm Class Interview of your students?*

- *How might you interest a colleague to work with you on peer review of teaching?*

9

CHANGE IS HARD IN ISOLATION BUT FACILITATED BY CONNECTIONS

Connecting on Campus

Changing the way you teach is hard in isolation, for many reasons, as we'll see. It is important, therefore, that you make connections with people who can help you, even if that means you are all learning together. This is Stage 5 of the stages of concern about innovation (shown earlier in Table 4.1), collaboration: "I am concerned about relating what I am doing with what other instructors are doing." It is taking another step in your development as a teacher. Those connections can be within your department, elsewhere on campus, or off campus either within your discipline or outside it. To make these connections, you have to let people know what you are doing or what you did. Therefore, while you are changing the way you teach your course, I urge you to keep a log, journal, or notebook of what you do (Brookfield, 1995, Teaching Logs). Think of it as the teaching equivalent of a lab notebook. It could be part of your teaching portfolio (Davis, 1993, Teaching Dossier; Seldin, 2004).

You may think that you would have more than enough to do just preparing for the classroom and carrying out those plans, let alone take time to make some notes. But you will soon forget many of the alterations you had to make, such as plans that didn't work, unexpected conflicts, or a need to stretch out or compress the schedule at a particular time, not to mention those stray ideas that flit through our minds at the unexpected call of our imagination. Ten minutes of reflective writing in that journal after each class meeting is not much time taken away from your other responsibilities. Besides, if you are like me, you will need at least half an hour to stem the rush of adrenaline from the excitement of the class. Take that time to write about what happened, should have happened, or shouldn't have happened during the class, before the class started, or after it was over.

During the term break following your course, I urge you to review those notes and collect them into a summary of the course that not only records what you did but what you didn't do, what worked, what didn't work and why, the alterations you made and why, and, most important, what changes you should make for the next time you teach the course and why. My report was 13 pages, single spaced. Owing to the significance of the projects to the students' grades for the course, I described the projects in detail. Those descriptions formed the basis for the changes I made the next year. Of the five projects (plus a bonus project) I used the first year, only three were kept for the next year, another one was altered, one was replaced, and one was dropped. In summarizing the information from my daily notes, I not only recorded descriptions but tried to come up with answers to the question: Why? This being my first attempt at such reflection, many of my answers were shallow. Nevertheless, they formed the beginning. However many changes you decide to make for the next term, having a record of your thoughts from the year before can be of immense help. An excellent guide for deepening this daily and summative reflection, beyond what I was capable of when I began, is the list of 13 questions on "how best to help and encourage people to learn" that were raised in a survey of "the best college teachers" (Bain, 2004, p. 60).

Once you have written the summary of your teaching in the course, you have a choice of what to do with it: either keep it to yourself or share the information with other faculty. You may decide merely to set it aside until you begin preparing for the course again and put in another term of teaching to add improvements. In so doing, you restrict the application of your experience to your course. You may think that a good idea, if you had many problems in the class. But talking to people about what you did is a better way to make improvements. The comfortable habit of our seclusion in the classroom, a habit that slights the discussion of what takes place in our classrooms, will tempt you to keep your results to yourself. And, yes, habits are hard to break, but by the end of your first term you will already have cracked that habit profoundly.

There is yet another hazard to your development as a teacher that comes from keeping your results to yourself: As Covey (1990) remarks,

"When we're left to our own experiences, we constantly suffer from a shortage of data" (p. 277). In private, it is easy for any of us to think we are better at what we do than we actually are. Brookfield (1995) warns of this:

> The intrinsic problem with approaches to private self-reflection is that when we use them, we can never completely avoid the risks of denial and distortion. We can never know just how much we're cooking the data of our memories and experience to produce images and renditions that show us off to good effect. (p. 33)

In other words, we can simply be human and succumb to the Lake Wobegon Effect (sometimes spelled "Lake Woebegone Effect") made famous by the humorist Garrison Keillor, in which most members of a group will rate themselves above average, or be so rated by doting others. One of the first documentations of this effect in faculty self-assessment of teaching was made by K. Patricia Cross, a leader in higher education. While on sabbatical at a research university, she asked the faculty to rate themselves as teachers. The results: 94% rated themselves as above average teachers and 68% rated themselves in the top quartile in teaching performance (Cross, 1977).

To recognize that this is a human, not a faculty, failing we have but to look at the annual survey of more than 200,000 students that is administrated during freshman orientations or the first week of classes at more than 400 four-year colleges and universities and that is coordinated by the Higher Education Research Institute at UCLA. For the academic years 2000–2001 through 2003–2004, the percent of students who rated themselves above average or in the highest 10% in academic ability increased each year, from 67% to 70%. (Highlights of the survey results are published each year in a January issue of *The Chronicle of Higher Education*.) The Lake Wobegon Effect is very robust, affecting all types of groups on all types of characteristics (Huff, 1998). The effect can most easily be guarded against by sharing reflective assessment of yourself with other members of the group for their feedback to you.

For the moment, however, I must put aside the benefits to be reaped from sharing your accomplishments with your colleagues and mention one reason you may not want to share the information: faculty resistance. If you are a junior faculty member, in particular if you have not yet attained tenure, and if the senior faculty in your department are known to oppose innovative teaching, then be discreet in sharing the results of your teaching experience. This warning goes double if you are a young woman faculty member and the senior faculty are old men, resistant to change. In such a situation the senior faculty have been known to condemn the young woman for using active learning, as they believe it "coddles students," whereas had she been a man, she would have "stood up in front of the class and told them what they ought to know." So be careful. Know the politics of your department. I second Weimer's (2002) recommendation: "If you are old, tenured, and without much to lose, go forth and win the resistance war for the rest of us. But if you are not, do not ignore the political realities of your situation" (p. 163). (As for me, I was a full professor, near retirement; they couldn't lay a hand on me.)

I am going to assume that sharing your experience will not harm your position. If things in your course went well, then you will be bubbling with excitement. You'll want to shout: LISTEN TO WHAT I DID! I HAD THE GREATEST TIME TEACHING THAT I'VE EVER HAD. I WANT YOU TO FEEL WHAT I FELT. It's the same surge of emotion that Covey (1990) cites in his class: "We became so excited about what was happening that . . . we all sensed an overwhelming desire to share what was happening with others" (p. 266). It's what one of my students wrote on the course evaluation: "I was excited about the material. I would leave class and would talk about both the material and the class format to anyone who would listen." It's a yearning for Palmer's (1998) "dialogue": "The growth of any craft depends on shared practice and honest dialogue among the people who do it" (p. 144). It's an essential step in establishing Brookfield's (1995) "critical conversations about teaching": "Critical reflection is an irreducibly social process" (p. 141). It is a novice's entrance into the "scholarship of teaching" (proposed by Boyer, 1990): "For a scholarship of teaching, we need scholarship that makes our work public and thus susceptible to critique. It then becomes community property, available for others to build upon" (Shulman, 1999, p. 16). Besides, it is what we do when we have finished writing the results of our research. We want to let people know what we have found and what we have concluded—except that the pleasure I received from my research results never burned with such intensity. But please note my choice of words: "surge of emotion," "yearning," "essential step," "entrance." This was the "Look-what-I-did!" stage. The "What-does-it-all-mean?" stage would come only with self-reflection and feedback.

I must confess that I couldn't wait until the end of the course to tell people what I was doing. I was about to burst with delight. So I took a very unusual step for me. That term I happened to be the coordinator for the weekly brown-bag lunch seminar for the marine geology and geophysics group of the School of Oceanography. I scheduled myself to be the speaker for the second week of the term—yes, the second week; I said I couldn't wait—to talk about my class, in which the students had just finished the first of their class periods on teaching the solutions to problems they had solved. (Many a time I had been cajoled into giving a seminar, but I cannot recall ever having volunteered to give one before.) The lunch seminar was listed in the school's weekly newsletter, which was also sent to several other departments. Normally the seminar attracted two dozen or so faculty and graduate students.

On that Thursday, I was the first one to the seminar room. I set up the overhead projector, placed my notes and the overhead transparencies in order, and waited, from chair to chair, to window, to water cooler in the hall, to chair, for people to arrive. When it was five minutes past the starting time and I realized that only eight people would hear me, my enthusiasm drained away, but after I began talking about the course, it surged back. (That surge returns like the tide every time I talk about the course, even to this day.)

The dean of the college was one of the attendees, which was very gratifying, but it was the stranger in the room who was about to give my life another lift. She turned out to be the director of a federally funded educational outreach program at the university and, more important, she taught a community college evening class in which she used cooperative learning. Not only was she the only person in the room who understood what I was trying to do, but she had been doing it for some time. So, something as minor as a brown-bag talk began my connections on campus. Use whatever method you can to let people know what you are doing.

A month later, when I was feeling the need for more advice and guidance, she introduced me to a faculty member in the College of Education who had helped her, a professor who worked with elementary and preservice teachers. And thus it came about that I met someone who understood what I was trying to do, taught in that format, and also knew the underlying pedagogical concepts and research. My discussions with her were very rewarding. She was the sole voice to commend me for my efforts that I could appreciate both for the kindness and encouragement that also characterized other voices and for the experience and expertise underpinning those words. It was from her that I first realized the magnitude of the reform movement in K–12 and undergraduate education that was underway in this country, particularly in science education— and I, me, with my head down, concentrating on what was in front of my nose, as I put together a new form of teaching in my own little course, was a part of it. When she told me I was a pioneer, I could but laugh in disbelief. To my way of thinking, this highly structured guy was the least likely person to be—a pioneer. Receiving her commendation further energized me, while at the same time it all but overwhelmed me.

When fall quarter was over, I began writing my summary of the course and completed it before the first of the New Year. Now I felt the need to spread the word about the course even farther. Put it down to the joyous energy of a new convert. What could I do to accomplish that goal during winter term? The answer came by email, a message seeking volunteers for the weekly afternoon seminar series attended by the entire School of Oceanography faculty and graduate students. Knowing that it was always difficult to find speakers early in a term, I volunteered and was gratefully accepted by the seminar coordinator. (In the time of three months I had volunteered to give two talks. Unthinkable! I had become a motor mouth, and proud of it—now that I had something to say that I wanted people to listen to.)

I did not think it prudent of me to plan a regular seminar talk, standing at the overhead projector, showing overhead transparencies, and—in effect—lecturing. I had made that mistake at the brown-bag lunch talk. No, this seminar had to be different. For one thing, there had never been a talk in this seminar series about teaching and learning since I had been on the faculty, and probably not before that either. I had no idea how the faculty and graduate students would receive it. Not many people had attended my brown-bag lunch talk. Would a similarly low turnout be my fate this time, too? I had to use my imagination and I had to leave the lectern. (Can you believe that? Look at what I just said. I'm using my imagination to plan a seminar—for crying out loud!—just as I had used my imagination in my course. My imagination and creativity were being released along paths they had never taken before. And they, in turn, were releasing a latent excitement.)

I emailed the students who had been in my course and asked for volunteers to present the seminar with me. That is, I had the audacity to ask those seniors to stand up in front of perhaps 80 to 90 faculty and graduate students, if we were lucky, people who were the teachers and TAs in the courses they had taken and would take, and to talk about how they had enjoyed a way of teaching that those faculty and graduate students might never attempt, nor perhaps even deem sound. I was asking a lot of them, but then I had asked a lot of them in the course—and they had mastered that challenge. I waited, hoping some of them would volunteer. And then the emails began arriving. I took the first four students to respond and thanked the next two for their willingness and let all the rest know not to respond. Then I invited the faculty member in the College of Education who had encouraged and advised me. She suggested I also invite an assistant provost who was active in education. He accepted. Pushing my luck, I even increased the time for the seminar from 50 minutes to an hour and a half, an unprecedented increase that risked dissuading people from attending.

On that Wednesday afternoon, the crowded lecture hall delighted me. One faculty member estimated the number of people to be half again the usual number for those seminars. The education professor spoke for 15 minutes about trends in education; the assistant provost spoke for 15 minutes about the process of change in education; I spoke for 15 minutes about the format of my course; and the four students spoke for a total of 15 minutes about the students' perspective of the course. Then for the discussion period, each speaker went to a corner of the room, with the students together in one corner, and people were invited to approach any of us for discussion of the topics. After perhaps 15 to 20 minutes, the education professor and the assistant provost were finished with questioners and waved me their goodbyes. After another 10 or 15 minutes I had no more people around me for discussion, but the students were still deep in several discussions.

I learned then that your students can be your best ambassadors for carrying the word about a different way of teaching to your faculty colleagues. An email to me the next day from a faculty member underscored that observation. He wrote, "Although I really enjoyed your presentation of the technique, the most impressive part was the talks by the undergraduates. Having four undergrads (even seniors) who are able to stand up in front of the full departmental seminar and make clear, articulate presentations impressed me (and the rest of the audience)."

Since one of the four students was scared to death of public speaking and since each student had had to give but one talk in my class and that was impromptu, I must assume that the power of their presentations was an affirmation of their experience in the course. Needless to say, I was immensely proud of those students—and, as it would turn out, the five of us were not through collaborating. Thus it was that with the help of others, I informed the faculty and graduate students in the school of a new way to teach.

It is important as well to look outside your department at other units on campus, both to let people know what you are doing and to learn more about teaching and learning. If a teaching/learning center is present, the consultants there can help you. They have experience in faculty development, and they know the literature on various aspects of teaching and learning. In addition, your institution may have a teaching institute for faculty to improve their teaching or it may offer workshops on teaching and learning. Any of these opportunities can connect you with other faculty at your institution who share your interest in changing the way to teach.

Connecting in Your Discipline

You should also look off campus for connections in your discipline. Having learned about cooperative learning at The Meeting in my discipline that I described in Chapter 4, I kept in touch by email through a listserv for attendees. In fact, at about the time I gave my brown-bag lunch talk, I emailed the leaders of The Meeting with a report of what I had accomplished since then. (All the attendees had been asked to submit such a report.) Since The Meeting I had become aware that several of the people who had attended were authorities in undergraduate education in the discipline. Therefore, I was surprised and delighted when one of these authorities invited me to submit a manuscript on teaching my course as part of a special issue on "teaching undergraduates in small groups" that she was coordinating for the education journal in the discipline. I eagerly accepted the invitation, but on one condition—that the four students who had participated in the seminar could submit a short companion paper that presented the students' perspective. The condition was accepted, and a few months later we sent off the two manuscripts as another partnership effort for the course. My manuscript, of course, was based on the report I had written over the Christmas break. The two papers soon appeared in print (Housel, Huston, Martin, & Pierce, 1995; McManus, 1995), thereby connecting me through the education journal in my discipline with colleagues in my discipline who were interested in innovative teaching. I urge you to examine a copy of the education journal in your discipline. Table 9.1 lists some of them.

Table 9.1

Some Education Journals in Various Disciplines of Higher Education

Education Journal	Sponsoring Organization
Art Education: The Journal of the National Art Education Association	National Art Education Association
Biochemistry and Molecular Biology Education	American Society of Biochemistry and Molecular Biology
Cell Biology Education	American Society for Cell Biology
Communication Education	National Communication Association
Discourse: Learning and Teaching in Philosophical and Religious Studies	American Association of Philosophy Teachers
The History Teacher	Society for History Education
Journal for Research in Mathematics Education	National Council of Teachers of Mathematics
Journal of Chemical Education	American Chemical Society
Journal of College Science Teaching	National Science Teachers Association
Journal of Engineering Education	American Society for Engineering Education
Journal of Geoscience Education	National Association of Geoscience Teachers
Journal of Resources and Life Sciences Education	American Society of Agronomy
The Physics Teacher	American Association of Physics Teachers
PS: Political Science & Politics (Teacher Section)	American Political Science Association
Teaching of Psychology	Society for the Teaching of Psychology
Teaching Sociology	American Sociological Association

It's funny: We have read our scholarly or research journals for years, commonly without a clue that an education journal even exists in our discipline. Yet in it you can find papers by faculty who teach the same concepts, methods, and applications as you, and their papers often present their solutions to the same teaching problems that you have encountered. Just as you can build on the results of their work, so too others can build on the results of your work, if you will but share those results. (If you happen to belong to a professional society that combines papers on education and research in the same journal, such as in the *Bulletin of the Ecological Society of America*, you do not have to search for an education journal.)

Writing papers is not the only way to connect in your discipline. That same spring that I was invited to write the paper, the professor whose five-page jigsaw handout at The Meeting had sparked my change invited me to become a distinguished speaker for the teaching society in my discipline during the next academic year. I would have to be willing to visit the department at any college or university that invited me to talk about how I had changed the format of my course. To be invited by an authority such as her flabbergasted me. You better believe that I accepted—but, again, on one condition: that a student could go with me to present the students' perspective. The condition was accepted very graciously, in spite of the extra cost for the student's travel. And thus began three years of travel, for the two of us much of the time, to a variety of institutions: liberal arts colleges, comprehensive universities, and research universities, at which I gave a talk or we gave a workshop and at which I learned from the experiences of faculty and students at those institutions. Visiting other institutions, particularly those that are not the same kind as yours—for me those were liberal arts colleges and comprehensive universities—enlightens you about the similarities and differences in teaching and learning within your discipline.

Although during the summer I worked as a visiting scientist with the faculty member from the College of Education in her research project to enhance elementary science education and by so doing learned something about the teaching challenges faced by elementary science teachers, I did not enhance my knowledge of cooperative learning. I had not yet sought out the teaching center. Therefore, instead of learning more about the hows and whys of the new way I was teaching and improving my teaching ability, I spent that time developing an end-of-program assessment of the undergraduate degree program for the School of Oceanography, at the director's request. And I helped the seniors put the research findings of their senior research projects on the web.

Having the assessment and the web on my mind, I gave a talk that fall on the end-of-assessment program at an education session of one national professional meeting in my discipline and a computer poster on the students' research postings at an education session of another national professional meeting in my discipline. These presentations formed the beginning of my presentations on undergraduate education at these meetings. Education sessions have grown in size and number at the annual meetings of professional organizations in many disciplines and provide another medium for exchanging experiences and ideas—that is, for connecting—about teaching in the discipline.

In association with one of those fall meetings, a small workshop was held on graduate education in the discipline. As a consequence of comments that I made there, one of the leaders of the workshop nominated me to be a member of the education committee of the organization. I accepted and by the following fall was organizing education sessions for the annual meetings of the organization. Attending workshops is yet another path for connecting with people in your discipline who want to enhance education in it.

There was a workshop at the other meeting that fall, too. At this one, however, I was one of the workshop leaders, the junior leader, rather than a participant. The professor who had invited me to submit a manuscript and the professor who had invited me to be a distinguished speaker had invited me to join them and two other colleagues for a workshop on innovative teaching in the discipline. These workshops at national meetings continued for several years and I had the pleasure of working with four accomplished innovative teachers, from whom I learned much about teaching that I applied in my course. Three of them were from liberal arts colleges and one was from a research university at which teaching was given more than passing notice. Two of them would be honored for their teaching as Carnegie Professor of the year for their states. In addition to the one-day workshops at meetings, we also held longer workshops in the

summers. I was fortunate to be able to work with these excellent teachers and with faculty from all types of institutions of higher education who came to the workshops to enhance their teaching and their students' learning.

By now it should be obvious that your discipline bears several pathways for learning more about changing the way you teach and building on the change. For as long as the only interest we have in the discipline is the content, in the form of the research, these pathways for connecting to our colleagues about education go unnoticed. But once you begin seeking them, you will find them, and you will find like-minded colleagues along the way.

Connecting Outside Your Discipline

In addition to the opportunities to connect with other faculty members by searching within your discipline, you can also find workshops held by general organizations that are outside your discipline. These organizations may comprise institutions of higher education, such as the Association of American Colleges and Universities (http://www.aacu-edu.org/) or they may be organizations dedicated to higher education, such as the Professional and Organizational Development Network in Higher Education (http://www.podnetwork.org/). You can find a description of the workshops offered by viewing the organizations' web sites and by looking at the Monthly Conference Calendar of the National Teaching and Learning Forum, online edition (http://www.ntlf.com). Individual institutions also offer summer workshops, such as The Evergreen State College through its Washington Center for Improving the Quality of Undergraduate Education (http://www.evergreen.edu/washcenter/home.htm). These workshops very commonly require that an institution send a team of persons. But some workshops are open to individual applicants. And for graduate students, there are the courses and experiences of the Preparing Future Faculty Programs (http://www.preparing-faculty.org/).

The major benefit from participating in one of these workshops is that you meet faculty from diverse disciplines and become aware of the

challenges that they are facing. It broadens your perspective of higher education. It was at one of these workshops that I received the first copy of a form for students to use in evaluating the progress of their group. It came from an English faculty member at a community college. I later found that my students had the same reaction to it as hers, which gave me an unexpected sense of satisfaction. Although there were several aspects of teaching that all participants in that workshop had experienced, there were also aspects that divided us by clusters of disciplines. For instance, the science faculty were drawn together by the challenge of teaching quantitative reasoning.

There is a significant difference between participants at an education workshop and a disciplinary research workshop. Regardless of how diverse the disciplines of the participants in an education workshop, we have many common experiences in the classroom and with students. Therefore, unlike a meeting of researchers in the discipline who share some general knowledge but are separated by the depth of their specialties, educators do not need background talks to set a context for the workshop. Educators can start discussing the topic right away, owing to shared experience. This commonality makes for spontaneous group work—except for the novice, whose feelings will probably mirror mine from my first meeting, The Meeting. Commonality also makes for a ready sharing of ideas and methods for the classroom. We borrow from one another without hesitation, but we usually have to make some adjustment to a borrowed method.

Connecting to Greater Depths

You may become so taken with the greater understanding of teaching you have gained from the change in the way you teach that you will begin asking deeper questions about your students' learning. Just knowing how to apply a teaching technique will no longer suffice, as I discovered after realizing a couple of years later that I didn't know how to help my faculty colleagues change the way they taught, if they did not choose to teach

as I taught. This disquietude grew within me, as I'll explain in the next chapter. My questions led me to two subjects: to me as a teacher in my discipline and to me as a teacher in general. We'll briefly consider each of these in turn.

At first I sought a deeper understanding of myself as a teacher in my discipline. I think each of us is aware that there are concepts, ideas, assumptions, and processes in our discipline that students have difficulty understanding, but we do not know how to help our students understand them. And we know that students enter our classes with misconceptions about the subject matter they will be taught by us, misconceptions that have helped them make some sense out of their world, but we tend to ignore those misconceptions and assume that because we have taught them "this content," then "this content" will replace any misconception they had.

Alas! We have but matched their misconception about content with our misconception about teaching. For that replacement does not occur 1) without a well-prepared procedure—for instance, bridging "students' correct beliefs . . . to their misconceptions through a series of intermediate analogous situations" (Bransford, Brown, & Cocking, 1999, p. 167) or using interactive lecture demonstrations with results that must be in real time (Bransford et al.), 2) without recognition that memory is a construction rather than an absorption, and 3) without considerable effort on the part of the instructor (Bain, 2004, Knowledge Is Constructed, Not Received). With minor modification, the following quotation could apply to my discipline and yours:

> As is well known, students enter their first physics course possessing strong beliefs and intuitions about common physical phenomena. These notions are derived from personal experience and color students' interpretations of material presented in the introductory course. Haloun and Hestenes [1985] show that instruction does little to change these 'common-sense' beliefs. (Mazur, 1997, p. 4)

You, likewise, may want to learn how to become a better teacher of the material in your discipline, and that means tackling some of the problems that beset students when, in order to learn the material in your course, they attempt to connect it to their existing academic knowledge and to their experience from everyday life. The challenge is enormous, as shown, for instance, by the research of the Physics Education Group at the University of Washington (http://www.phys.washington.edu/groups/peg/). But the alternative is that students can pass exams, homework problems, and courses without truly understanding and retaining what they memorized for their grades. Although I realized that answering this challenge would be a major contribution to education in my discipline, the research required is so labor intensive that I chose to follow another path, learning more about myself as a teacher in general.

As a teacher, I now realized that although I could perform a teaching technique, I did not know the rationale behind the technique. Nor did I know the most efficient or effective way to use the technique. What I knew was what I did, and what I did differed in some ways from the instructions on that five-page jigsaw handout from The Meeting. I accepted that other faculty could teach by a jigsaw differently from me, but I had little advice to guide them beyond my experience. I felt the need for a deeper understanding of the teaching techniques I was using. Therefore, I stopped giving workshops and began to study teaching and learning.

Reflective Questions

- *In what ways can you inform the faculty in your department about your change in teaching?*

- *Is it politically prudent for you to inform your colleagues?*

- *How might your students help you make connections?*

- *Does your library have the education journal in your discipline?*

- *What kinds of papers are presented in the education sessions at meetings of the organizations in your discipline?*

- *If the meetings have no education sessions, what is the procedure to propose one?*

- *How can you find out what education workshops are held in your discipline?*

- *How could you discover what misconceptions students hold about the material you teach?*

10

CHANGE MEANS CHANGING YOUR CONCEPTS ABOUT EDUCATION

The Need for a Frame of Reference

Let me back up a bit in my story, to a time shortly after I made the decision to retire, when one of my former students came to see me. She had been in the first class I taught by cooperative learning. After extending her regrets for the end of my teaching and congratulations on my coming retirement, she asked whom I had trained to take my place teaching the course. I replied, "No one," since that was a decision for the director and the faculty. She wanted to know if the course would continue to be taught by cooperative learning, and I said, "Probably not." There was silence. Eyes narrowed, tongue sharpened to slice off the words, she said, "So! You teach the best course I ever had, and now you're just going to quit. Like that! Don't you have any sense of responsibility? Don't you care?" In my befuddlement I reverted to an earlier mode of reaction, "Why is this student talking to me like this?"

It came about that soon thereafter I sent out an email message to the faculty, inviting them to attend my course on the next Tuesday or Wednesday. They could spend as long as they wanted in the classroom, sit with the students, listen to the groups, whatever; they would not—in fact, were not able to—disturb us. A handful did come, and one of them gave me the best compliment I ever received on the course. She said in amazement, "I've never seen a college course like this. It reminds me of my daughter's third-grade class." I was deeply grateful, for as you may recall, cooperative learning, and indeed the jigsaw structure (Aronson, Blaney, Stephan, Sikes, & Snapp, 1978), originated in the elementary schools. That such a positive learning environment from elementary school would seem amazing in a college classroom is, sadly, ironic.

Later in the term, I invited the faculty to meet for an hour to learn

139

more about cooperative learning. Once again there was a turnout of six or eight people. We had an interesting discussion, but it brought home to me that the only teaching format I knew how to use was *my* jigsaw format. (For other formats, see Aronson et al. [1978] and Clarke [1994].) That was the workshop I gave on my visits to other institutions and at meetings of professional societies in my discipline. Most of these workshops were attended by faculty who wanted to change the way they taught. My colleagues, however, were merely curious about the way I was teaching. Although I knew something about other innovative ways to teach from having listened to other workshop leaders, I did not know enough to teach someone who was merely curious about how to teach with those formats, and it seemed obvious to me that my colleagues were not interested in teaching with my jigsaw. As a result, my meager efforts, as I mentioned in the last chapter, generated little change in the faculty's way of teaching.

The unintended result of my efforts to introduce other faculty in my department to cooperative learning was to enclose me in a loneliness that I would later discover to be a common part of teaching (Jersild, 1955; Kraft, 2002). What I needed was

> the guidance that a community of collegial discourse
> provides—to say nothing of the support such a com-
> munity can offer to sustain me in the trials of teaching
> and the cumulative and collective wisdom about this
> craft that can be found in every faculty worth its salt.
> (Palmer, 1998, p. 142)

It took three years before my needs were met, by the good fortune of my becoming a faculty associate in the Center for Instructional Development and Research at the University of Washington. In the "community of collegial discourse" that I found there, in the experience of working with faculty and graduate students from other departments who came there as clients seeking to improve their teaching, and in the literature on faculty development and pedagogy in their library, I learned a great deal about teaching and learning and about myself as a teacher. Most important for my own development, I realized that I lacked a frame of reference for my teaching. I was practiced in the use of one technique, but how did that technique fit into something grander, something that connected with my other experiences as a faculty member, such as mentoring and advising, something that gave me an understanding of my relationship to other faculty members, and something that gave a context to my thoughts about teaching? I soon discovered the frame of reference that I needed: the paradigms of education.

Paradigms of Education

I discovered that several authorities had written about paradigms of education, for example, Barr and Tagg (1995), Garvin (1991), Johnson, Johnson, and Smith (1991), Meyers and Jones (1993), and Smith and Waller (1997). Education paradigms are frames of reference that determine the way we perceive, interpret, and make sense out of how we educate our students (Johnson et al.). By the time I had finished studying these writings (McManus, 2001), I felt that I had indeed made sense out of how we educate our students.

Two education paradigms are usually described: one we may call the teaching-centered paradigm and the other the learning-centered paradigm. Let me emphasize at the outset that teaching and learning occur under both paradigms. The operational difference between them is one of emphasis. As their names imply, under one the emphasis is on faculty teaching, that is, on what the instructor does; under the other the emphasis is on student learning, that is, on what the students do. The teaching-centered paradigm is the one under which we began teaching by lecturing to classes of note-taking students. It is the conventional or traditional paradigm with which we are all familiar. The learning-centered paradigm is the paradigm under which cooperative learning is a teaching method.

The teaching-centered paradigm carries with it the ironic annotation that it is not usually recognized as a paradigm by faculty teaching under it. Rather, this kind of teaching, which I described in Chapter 1, is thought of as just doing what we ought to do. The paradigm remains "invisible" (Barr & Tagg, 1995, p. 25), because it is so "deeply ingrained in each of us" (Meyers & Jones, 1993, p. 15) that it has become the "context in which [we] live" (Smith & Waller, 1997, p. 277). It is like "a force of nature" (Barr & Tagg, p. 25). By contrast, the learning-centered paradigm with all its difference from what we are used to is clearly defined as a paradigm. That designation can make it appear artificial when contrasted to the conventional, invisible paradigm.

A contrast of these two paradigms is usually limited to the teaching methods, normally phrased as the contrast between lecturing to passive students and enabling students to learn actively. But the contrasts are more fundamental than that, beginning with the assumptions that the two paradigms make about education. Table 10.1 is a highly abbreviated list that contrasts several characteristics of the two paradigms. There are other characteristics. A discussion of these contrasts, based on the references cited in Table 10.1, plus Tagg (2003), can help us understand our natural resistance to changing the way we teach.

Table 10.1

Abbreviated Contrast of Several Characteristics of the Two Paradigms of Education

Assumptions about education	• Content is primary and instructor owns the knowledge	• Process of learning is as important as content learned
	• Instructor is central	• Instructor and students are partners
	• Learning is cumulative	• Learning is a dynamic process of restructuring
	• Students enter class with empty minds	• Students enter class with a perceptual framework intact
	• Students differ little from instructor	• Many students differ from instructor
	• Success is an individual accomplishment	• Success results from teamwork

Educational goals	• Instructor transfers information to students	• Instructor creates a learning environment
	• Students accumulate knowledge	• Students develop skills in constructing and using knowledge
Assessment of results	• Students are assessed infrequently by exams on knowledge of content	• Students are assessed frequently with classroom assessment techniques
Teaching methods	• Lecturing	• Active learning and lecturing
Classroom environments	• Competitive and individualistic	• Collaborative, cooperative, and supportive of learning, risk-taking
Instructor's responsibilities	• Be current in knowledge of content	• Be current in knowledge of content
	• Present content	• Possess pedagogical content knowledge
Instructor-students relationship	• Impersonal, little interaction	• Personal, partnership between instructor and students

Note. Adapted from "The two paradigms of education and the peer review of teaching" by D. A. McManus, 2001, *Journal of Geoscience Education, 49*, pp. 425–426, which was adapted and compiled from Barr and Tagg (1995); Garvin (1991); Johnson, Johnson, and Smith (1991); Meyers and Jones (1993); and Smith and Waller (1997). Copyright 2001 by National Association of Geoscience Teachers. Adapted with permission.

Resistance to Change

For the familiar teaching-centered paradigm, the principal assumption is that content is primary, which is not surprising, because knowledge of content in our discipline was the measure of our education and is the basis for our prestige in research. No wonder we value content so highly.

It is, with little exaggeration, all we know. To diminish the value of content even slightly seems to diminish our self-assurance and self-esteem. Who wants to do that? It threatens us. It raises anxiety.

Yet, that is what the learning-centered paradigm demands of us, for the principal assumption of that paradigm is that learning, the process of forming knowledge, is as important as the content learned; in other words, students must learn both the content and how to learn and use the content (see Bain, 2004, What Do They Know About How We Learn?). And that implies that we have to know more than just content. Another threat! More anxiety! It's natural to resist. We can conceal our anxiety by declaring that we cannot cut content and use the time so freed to teach students how to learn and use the content, because all the content we teach is important for the students to know. I certainly implied to students that everything I had covered in my lectures was important for them to know.

Although content in the discipline is certainly important—students have to learn some content—we now know from research on education and research on learning that under the teaching-centered paradigm seniors and alums deem content in the discipline less important for success in life after college than developing learning skills (Chapter 7), that students retain little understanding of content in a course (Chapter 6), that content in courses should be reduced categorically (Chapter 6), that we limit the amount of content in a course anyway (Chapter 6), and that, according to Bain (2004), the best teachers emphasize "helping people learn to reason or create, to use information, not tell[ing] students everything they must know and understand" (p. 51). These research findings can cause us anxiety under the teaching-centered paradigm, but as Johnson (1998) reminds us, "The fear *you let* build up in your mind is worse than the situation that actually exists" (p. 63). You can make the change. You can weed out content.

Furthermore, there is good evidence that we develop as a teacher (Nyquist & Wulff, 1996; Weimer, 2002, Taking a Developmental Approach). According to Weimer, "There is a general sense in the literature that as teachers mature, they move from an almost exclusive content orientation to a more student-centered approach" (p. 178). As in the stages of concern about innovation (shown earlier in Table 4.1), the emphasis changes from what the teacher does and how those actions affect him or her to what the students do and how what the teacher does affects the students. If you have arrived at this advanced stage of development as a teacher, you will overcome your resistance more readily, and the change will be that much easier for you.

Under the teaching-centered paradigm (see Table 10.1), we comfortably assume that students enter our classes with "empty minds" because then all we have to do is fill those minds with content, or if the analogy should be "minds like sponges," then we merely provide them content to soak up. Content! Content! Content! Isn't that assumption deeply ingrained in you? Furthermore, we treat the students as though they are all alike, they are like we were as students, and they learn the way we learned, or think we learned—and we future professors learned content.

All these assumptions place the emphasis on the instructor's providing content: One lecture fits all, with little need for interaction between us and the students, an impersonal condition that resulted in my not knowing the names of most students in my class for year after year when I taught under this paradigm. Hence the assumptions, and the educational goals that follow from them—to transfer information for the students to accumulate as knowledge—seem to be pure common sense. But as Brookfield (1995) warns us, "We fall into the habits of justifying what we do by reference to unchecked 'common sense' and of thinking that the unconfirmed evidence of our own eyes is always accurate and valid" (p. 4). So, since these assumptions and goals are not "common sense," but merely one set of assumptions and goals, we can replace them with another set of assumptions and goals. We are not—I repeat: not—violating a natural law.

According to the learning-centered paradigm, the students enter our classes with minds that, instead of being empty, contain perceptive frameworks to which the content we provide them must connect in order for them to learn it. And that requires us to have a personal relationship with the students, a requirement for getting to know the students and how they think that we are not used to honoring. The challenge is enormous, owing to its complexity, which derives from the students not being like we were as students. Let's look at three aspects of the challenge to know our students.

First, when we began teaching, the students were the age of our younger siblings, and, therefore, somewhat like us. As the years have passed, the age of the students in our classes has not changed, but our age has. We know it has increased, but we can easily ignore the result of our aging: the age of our students, instead of being the age of our younger siblings, is now the age of our children or our grandchildren. Our students are no more like us than our children or grandchildren are. Woe to us if we treat them as though they were like us. More anxiety! (For eye-opening lists of distinctive characteristics of today's college students see publications such as McGuire & Williams [2002] and The Mindset List for entering freshmen prepared each year by Beloit College [http://www.beloit.edu].)

Second, and forming a major part of the challenge, many of the students come from cultural and social backgrounds different from ours, and their numbers can be expected to grow as they form an increasing percentage of the college-age population, becoming a majority by 2050 (National Science Foundation, 2004). Today these minorities are underrepresented in institutions of higher education (see American Council on Education, 2003) and badly underrepresented in such disciplines as mathematics, science, and engineering (see National Science Board, 2004). We must assume part of the blame for this underrepresentation, for we obviously have not engaged these students' interest in our disciplines as effectively as we should have. And if we are this ineffective today, when minorities form approximately one-third of the college-age population, and if we make no effort to change our teaching to engage the interest of all students, then how foreboding looms the future for our disciplines, both as part of the knowledge possessed by educated citizens and as a field of human scholarship!

Following the learning-centered paradigm can help us meet this aspect of the challenge. In addition to the references I have cited previously, a wealth of information on enhancing minority education is available on the web, under such headings as "diversity," "inclusive teaching," "minorities," and "multicultural teaching." For example, there are web sites of educational organizations—American Association for Higher Education (www.aahe.org/), American Council on Education (www.acenet.edu/), Association of American Colleges and Universities (www.aacu-edu.org/), among others. There are also web sites of professional organizations in your discipline, such as the American Association for the Advancement of Science "Minority Scientists Network" (http://nextwave.sciencemag.org/miscinet/) in science. And there are web sites of teaching centers, in particular see the Center for Instructional Development and Research (2004a), Center for Research on Learning and Teaching (2004), Derek Bok Center for Teaching and Learning (2002–2004), and Faculty Teaching Excellence Program (2004).

The third aspect of the challenge to know our students is that the way students learn is now thought to be different from the way we think we learned. That's another idea we are not comfortable with and can ignore as a teaching-centered instructor, but one we can deal with as a learning-centered instructor. Research on learning suggests that students do not just accumulate knowledge but construct their knowledge by restructuring their existing knowledge to incorporate the new information into new knowledge (Bransford, Brown, & Cocking, 1999). By appreciating how students learn, we can better interest students in the questions asked in our discipline and, through that process, come to know the students better.

All the assumptions listed earlier in Table 10.1 place the emphasis on a partnership of learning between instructor and students, which threatens our control of the class and naturally makes us anxious, as do the educational goals that follow from these assumptions: creating a learning environment and enhancing the students' skills in learning. These assumptions and goals require us to reflect on teaching and learning, to try to understand how our students learn, and to hone our skills for working with people.

Although we tend to say that we don't have time to learn skills—an excuse that we'll deal with in a moment—the truth is that we can learn the required skills in workshops and from consultants, and not all at once, as you have seen from my example. We can learn the required skills because we need to learn them if we want to join the "community of practice" (Brown & Duguid, 2000) under the learning-centered paradigm, and as Brown and Duguid further note, "People learn in response to need" (p. 136). When we have a need to know, nothing is as difficult to learn as we had imagined before the need arose. Besides, the skills we need to learn are the skills of the best teachers (Bain, 2004).

Underlying these different assumptions and goals, in my opinion, are two quite different defining principles of education. The teaching-centered instructor professes, "I teach [discipline name] to students and expect (want) them to learn it"—note the emphasis on content—whereas the learning-centered instructor professes, "I help students to learn, specifically to learn [discipline name], by the way I teach them"—note the emphasis on learning (McManus, 2001, p. 424). In Bain's (2004) survey of the best college teachers, he reports of those teachers that "rather than thinking just in terms of teaching history, biology, chemistry, or other topics, they talked about teaching students to understand, apply, analyze, synthesize, and evaluate evidence and conclusions" (p. 46).

The principle of teaching the discipline seems natural to us, familiar; the latter principle seems artificial, unfamiliar. These principles are not the end points of a gradation along which we can slide. (A sense of gradation can arise, though, from the unreflective cross-paradigm borrowing of teaching techniques. This borrowing is part of the widely reported disjunction between faculty educational goals and educational practice [Murray & MacDonald, 1997], which I certainly exhibited.) Rather, these principles represent two separate paradigms that can no more be held, even partially, by anyone at the same time than can the images of the two women in the visual illusion in Figure 10.1. (See Covey [1990, pp. 24–29] for further comparison of paradigms and visual illusions.)

Figure 10.1

Visual illusion of young woman with head turned toward her right shoulder and old woman with chin resting on her chest. (The young woman's left ear is the old woman's left eye.) The two women cannot be seen at the same time. Only one or the other can be seen. In the same way, only one paradigm of education can be held. Both cannot be held at the same time.

From such contrasting assumptions, goals, and defining principles there will naturally arise a need for different teaching methods, or different uses of the same method, to fulfill those assumptions, attain those goals, and be true to those principles, and different assessment tools to measure progress and results. We are all used to transferring content by lecturing for 50 minutes and giving a midterm and final exam for after-the-fact assessment of whether the content transferred can be repeated to us. But the learning-centered instructor may use lecturing for only 10 minutes or so before switching to a student activity and then assess the students' learning with a classroom assessment technique (Angelo & Cross, 1993) in order to revisit any part of the lesson that the students are having difficulty understanding so that their understanding can be improved.

Furthermore, the learning-centered instructor is also expected to be responsible for knowing how to teach the content so that students can learn it; that is, to have "pedagogical content knowledge" (Shulman, 1986, p. 9) of the discipline, and to set learning outcomes and goals for the course, set explicit standards for learning, and establish a supportive classroom environment. These are very different requirements from transferring content. When stated like this, they threaten us. It's natural to resist them, but the purpose of this book is to enable you to visualize a course taught with these methods, albeit imperfectly, and to prepare you to undertake the change, and by this example to reduce your anxiety.

Although the two competing paradigms of education are not precisely like the competing paradigms of scientific concepts studied by Kuhn (1996), they have many similarities; specifically they are incommensurable, in that they possess no common standard for comparison. According to Kuhn, it follows from this observation that "the proponents of competing paradigms must fail to make complete contact with each other's viewpoints" (p. 148). This failure to communicate across the divide unnecessarily heightens the perceived threat of the learning-centered paradigm, which is usually expressed only as a different teaching method, and therefore saps one's interest in attempting any change. But if we examine the three ramifications that follow from this failure in communication, we can recognize our resistance to change as too often an emotional response to what is a research-based, logically formulated, different framework that makes sense out of teaching differently.

The first ramification is that faculty who are teaching under the different paradigms hold different standards or definitions of education, as a result of which they "will often disagree about the list of problems that any candidate paradigm must resolve" (Kuhn, 1996, p. 148). Hence, it is only natural for the teaching-centered instructor to assert that, for a paradigm of education, "learning" is the students' responsibility, which in the main it is, and thereby to resist the learning-centered instructor's assertion that in part, as a partner, it is the teacher's responsibility. "It's my responsibility to teach; it's their responsibility to learn" is what I said, and believed for most of my years teaching. Besides, I really didn't know how to help students learn. But, the learning-centered instructor would ask, as I asked in the preface, if much about how students learn is now known from research, then why don't we use that knowledge to teach them in ways that enhance their learning? In our research we would certainly use our knowledge of how a natural process works in order to benefit users of the product of that process. Why not apply the same approach in our teaching? Why not learn to understand the process of learning so that we can benefit our student users of that process? This request does not seem unreasonable. Learning is not entirely the student's responsibility.

The second ramification is that the same vocabulary is used in different ways under the different paradigms. Take the term "classroom environment." To the teaching-centered instructor the classroom environment is one of competition and individualism. Students are expected to work and study alone amidst keen competition; they are graded competitively (on a curve); ability is assumed fixed and scarce (we tacitly subscribe to a scarcity mentality [Covey, 1990]); excellence by some students will weed out students of poorer performance. This may well be the only classroom environment we have ever known.

To the learning-centered instructor the classroom environment is one of collaboration and cooperation. Students are expected to work and study together for at least part of the time; they are graded against a standard, not against one another; ability is assumed generous and students are assumed capable of success; risk-taking in learning is encouraged; "weeding out," to use the same term, occurs by failing to meet the standard set for everyone, not by failing in competition. With such contrasting definitions of the same term, misunderstanding and suspicion of the new definition is to be expected, but now you have a rough idea from my experience of what the latter kind of classroom environment is like and the joy that it can bring to both you and your students.

The third, and as Kuhn (1996) notes, the most fundamental ramification of incommensurability is that "the proponents of competing paradigms practice their trades in different worlds" (p. 150). When instructors teaching under the two paradigms carry out the daily lesson, they do so within the quite different contexts of their paradigms. For the daily lesson under the teaching-centered paradigm, the instructor provides students with what he or she thinks they need to know about some content. Under the learning-centered paradigm, the instructor uses activities to enable students to learn by connecting new content to what they already know and then helps them to use skills they have learned in order to transfer the new knowledge to a new situation so as to understand that situation. Both instructors would say that the students are learning in their class, and both would be correct, but research supports the latter instructor's class as providing the better learning environment (Bain, 2004; Bransford et al., 1999; National Research Council, 2000). Isn't enabling our students to learn to the best of their ability what our teaching is really all about? And, yes, in the beginning it will take you more effort to teach in the world of the learning-centered classroom. Accommodating change takes effort. My example, however, suggests the kind of world it can be for you. Various resources can guide you into this new world (see Weimer, 2002, Implementing the Learner-Centered Approach).

Reflective Questions

- *What are one or two actions you take in your class that exemplify each assumption about education for the teaching-centered paradigm as listed in Table 10.1?*

- *Which of the assumptions about education for the learning-centered paradigm listed in Table 10.1 have you exemplified by actions taken in your class?*

- *If you were forced to reduce the credits for your course from three credits to two credits, say, to help make room for a new course in the curriculum, how would you go about reducing the amount of content?*

- *If you go to the home page for Beloit College (www.beloit.edu) and click on The Mindset List, which lists the cultural references for the students born 18 years previously—the majority of the entering freshman class—and read the list of the cultural references of these students, how does this list change your metaphors, analogies, intimations, or other attempts at trying to connect your information to the experiences and interests of those students?*

- *How do your course content and teaching methods welcome a diverse range of students?*

- *Pedagogical content knowledge is knowledge of the way to teach a particular aspect of your course so that the barrier to the students learning that aspect is lowered or removed. How many examples of your pedagogical content knowledge for your course can you list?*

11

CHANGE MEANS CHANGING YOUR CONCEPTS ABOUT YOURSELF

Familiar Excuses

We express our resistance to change in excuses. You may have uttered one or more of four familiar excuses for not changing the way you teach: 1) I don't have the time to change, 2) I can succeed without changing anything, 3) There is no reward for changing, or 4) It's all about good teaching, and good teaching can't be defined. On inspection, however, these excuses turn out to be hollow.

When a student tells you he or she "didn't have time" to do the homework for today and presents no credible evidence that an emergency obtruded to prevent completion of the task, what is your response? Precisely! It goes without saying. And yet, we may turn around and use the same excuse for not changing the way we teach. (But let funding for a new research initiative be announced and we can jolly well find the time both to be part of a proposal for funding and to make time for the new research activity, if funded.) "I just don't have the time" is part of the vocabulary of reactive people; "it absolves them of responsibility" (Covey, 1990, p. 78). It says that we are not controlling our lives; something "out there" is. So take charge of your life. If you want to change the way you teach, you will find the time to do it, just as you found the time to write that new research proposal.

To say that you can succeed in your job without changing the way you teach is not so much another excuse as a justification for doing nothing. And the fact is you stand a good chance of succeeding at a research university even though you are a poor teacher—if you receive external commendations and rewards for your research. The underlying issue, however, is whether you are content to be the teacher you are, rather than the one you could become. Why not envision yourself "finding something better—much better" (Johnson, 1998, p. 71)? You have read how much better my class was both for me and the students after the change, how much more enjoyable. Why not be able to say the same for your class? Why not enjoy it more?

The third and fourth excuses are connected: no reward and no definition of good teaching. In a research university you should not expect to be rewarded for changing your teaching any more than you should expect to be rewarded for good teaching or using promising practices of teaching, because the standards for good teaching are not discussed by the faculty and, therefore, are not recognized as such. The absence of discussion comes as no surprise. After all, under the invisible teaching-centered paradigm, the instructor's responsibility is to be current in knowledge of content, present the content accurately, clearly, and logically in a well-controlled classroom, and test the students for recall of the content.

This behavior has become such a habit that we assume all our colleagues are fulfilling this responsibility, this "force of nature," just as we declare we are. So, what standards of good teaching could there possibly be? No wonder discussion is absent. No wonder I have heard faculty declare, "You cannot define good teaching." And if the faculty cannot recognize good teaching—other than by accepting some number on the student ratings of the instructor at the end of the term—then there can be no serious reward for good teaching, let alone reward for changing the way we teach, for it is our department colleagues who recommend us for tenure, promotion, or merit increase in salary.

All is not bleak, however. In fact, things are indeed looking up. Faculty are now talking about teaching and learning, far more than in the past and in many more forums (Hutchings, 2004). New administrative structures for research on undergraduate education are springing up, such as the Institute for Transforming Undergraduate Education at the University of Delaware (http://www.udel.edu/inst/) and the Reinvention Center (for Undergraduate Education) at Stony Brook University (http://www.sunysb.edu/Reinventioncenter/), to name but two examples. (See the Appendix for other programs to enhance undergraduate teaching and learning.)

Furthermore, I want to make it clear that there are indeed characteristics of good teaching, which have been repeatedly identified through research. Perhaps the best known is the list of characteristics by Chickering and Gamson (1987):

- Good practice encourages contacts between students and faculty

- Good practice develops reciprocity and cooperation among students

- Good practice uses active learning techniques

- Good practice gives prompt feedback

- Good practice emphasizes time on task

- Good practice communicates high expectations

- Good practice respects diverse talents and ways of learning

Another list is by Bain (2004):

- Create a natural critical learning environment

- Get students' attention and keep it

- Start with the students rather than the discipline

- Seek commitments

- Help students learn outside of class

- Engage students in disciplinary thinking

- Create diverse learning experiences

Also see a checklist by Davis (1993, Viewing the Videotape), a noting of characteristics and references by Eble (1988), and a research report edited by Perry and Smart (1997). Think of the way you teach and then think back on my fumbling attempts during the year I changed. Which of those two ways of teaching more closely fits with the characteristics of good teaching listed above?

Not only can a faculty that is uninformed about good teaching not create a meritorious reward for teaching, neither can uninformed administrators, for administrators were faculty members first and have commonly done little to change their own perception of teaching under the teaching-centered paradigm. Yes, there are teaching awards, created by the administration, usually with a small honorarium, and to the credit of some awards only students who have taken the course that year can nominate an instructor for the award. But my opinion of teaching awards as motivation for faculty to improve their teaching is the same as that of cook-off awards as motivation for neighbors to improve their baking. In both cases, I believe the general attitude, of colleagues or neighbors, toward the recipient of the award is, "It's all about talent. Some people are born good teachers/cooks. Some are not. What does it have to do with me?" (By contrast, I think money spent on faculty development— and the administration's promotion of faculty development—could improve teaching.)

Since you are not likely to be rewarded for good teaching—as yet— you can either use this characteristic of research universities as an example of the rule that "you basically get what you reward" (Covey, 1990, p. 229) and therefore as ample justification for not changing your teaching, or you can accept the situation and change anyway, because you want to discover something about yourself as a teacher.

You as a Teacher

Teaching under the teaching-centered paradigm is a habit. We did not deliberately, or even voluntarily, accept those assumptions, goals, and other characteristics as the framework of our teaching. No one taught us to become teaching-centered instructors. In fact, no one taught us to teach. The first assumption for preparing to teach under the teaching-centered paradigm says it all (see Table 11.1): Master the content, for any expert can teach. Either we heard this said or it was implied by example. Today, a teaching-centered instructor is likely not only to exemplify this assumption but to inculcate it in his or her graduate students. Since, according to the teaching-centered paradigm, anyone who has mastered the content can teach it, there is no need for a department, or university, to have a program to teach graduate students how to teach. In this manner, the teaching-centered instructors have reproduced themselves effectively for a long, long time.

Table 11.1

Abbreviated Contrast of the Two Paradigms of Education for Preparation for Teaching and for Motivating and Mentoring Students

Characteristics	Teaching-Centered Paradigm	Learning-Centered Paradigm
Preparation for teaching	• Master the content—any expert can teach.	• Master the content.
	• Develop clear presentation of lectures.	• Develop interpersonal skills of questioning, listening, responding, and sensitivity to group processes.
		• Learn how to assess students' needs and levels of understanding. Develop pedagogical content knowledge.
	• Teaching is a routine activity.	• Teaching is complex and requires training.
Motivating and mentoring students	• Students are expected to be self-motivating.	• Help students learn how to set goals, establish a plan to achieve goals, and record progress.
		• Align students' intact motivation with course goals.
	• Mentoring consists of enhancing the learning of content.	• Mentoring consists of helping students become lifelong learners and turning majors from students into apprentices.

Note. From "The two paradigms of education and the peer review of teaching" by D. A. McManus, 2001, *Journal of Geoscience Education, 49,* pp. 425–426, which was adapted and compiled from Barr and Tagg (1995); Garvin (1991); Johnson, Johnson, and Smith (1991); Meyers and Jones (1993); and Smith and Waller (1997). Copyright 2001 by the National Association of Geoscience Teachers. Reprinted with permission.

By contrast, the learning-centered paradigm assumes that teaching is complex and requires training. As with the learning of any skill, we can learn to teach by ourselves, but learning from learning-centered instructors is more efficient. Hence, we find an increasing number of training programs to prepare graduate students, new faculty, and existing faculty to teach (see the Appendix).

A glance at Table 11.1 reveals how wide is the range of skills required for emphasizing student learning, far wider than just mastering the content, though mastering the content is, even for this paradigm, the prime requirement for teaching. Those courses I taught while I was learning the content would have been a complete disaster had I tried to leave the lectern, assuming I would have known about active learning at that time. The courses were bad enough with my lecturing. One has to know the content, and know it cold. The challenge is using that knowledge of content to help students learn.

Now notice the differences required of us by the two paradigms for motivating and mentoring students. Motivating and mentoring for the learning-centered instructor consists of helping the students, and helping them in a very personal way. Motivation is not left to the students' self-motivation. It is also our responsibility. Mentoring is not restricted to helping students learn content. It includes helping all students learn how to learn and helping our majors learn how to think and act as junior members of our profession. But as teaching-centered instructors, we expected our students to be self-motivated, as we fondly remember we were. It was a habitual way of regarding students.

So, we picked up a habit; and we picked up several more habits. We did what we thought we ought to do. (When I began teaching, I wore a white shirt and a tie to campus every day, because that was what the other male faculty wore. I picked up the habit, to fit in.) But habits can be broken, as we know. And we can appreciate Covey's (1990) reminder that breaking a habit "involves a process and a tremendous commitment" (p. 46) and that "change—real change—comes from the inside out . . . from striking at the root—the fabric of our thought" (p. 317). This is why we must examine "the fabric of our thought" about ourselves as teachers.

When I first read Parker Palmer's reflections on "the teacher within" (Palmer, 1998, The Teacher Within), I thought the whole thing too touchy-feely to take seriously. Listening to the voice of the teacher within? Come, now! But Palmer contrasts listening to this internal voice with listening to what the conditions around us say we "ought" to do, and he then asks of this "ought," "But is it my vocation? Am I gifted and called to do it?" (p. 30). He further asks, "How many teachers inflict their own pain on their students, the pain that comes from doing what never was, or no longer is, their true work?" (p. 30). I, for one, prefer not to recall those years when I taught as I thought I "ought" to.

Covey (1990) picks up the same theme when he notes that much of our life is shaped by default, by scripts written by other people, by circumstances, by conditions. It is clear to me that even we Ph.D.s can allow those conditions to control us, tell us what we ought to do—or we can decide what is best for us, regardless of the conditions. Those decisions are based on our values; that is to say, on "the way things should be" (p. 24), and in this instance, the way things should be for us as a teacher. And we are back to listening to the voice of the teacher within, which can tell us how things should be for us as a teacher.

You are probably asking yourself, "How do I hear that voice?" The question has been asked by others: "How does one attend to the voice of the teacher within?" (Palmer, 1998, p. 31). "How is voice discovered?" (Brookfield, 1995, p. 47). To say it is by reflection is to state the obvious. The challenge is for the reflection to connect within us. For me, the reflection occurred after I had taught my course by cooperative learning. Thinking back over the time from my Thursday afternoon special classes to my establishment of the jigsaw format of cooperative learning, I realize that at no time in making those innovations did I expect failure. Something deep inside me told me that I was doing what was right, at least for me. I throbbed with excitement, with energy. Now I understand why. On later reading the following passages describing the voice of the teacher within, my heart leaped in recognition:

> [It says things like,] "This is what fits you and this is
> what doesn't"; "This is who you are and this is who you
> are not"; "This is what gives you life and this is what
> kills your spirit—or makes you wish you were dead."
> (Palmer, 1998, p. 31)

> We hear our voice saying, "What I'm doing now is cre-
> ative and spontaneous, yet grounded in my examined
> experiences. I know it's good for me and for my stu-
> dents. What's more, I know why it's good and if need
> be I can tell you why." (Brookfield, 1995, p. 47)

When we are being true to ourselves, our integrity, our inner self—
call it what you will—we are happy. You have read about my years of lecturing. Those were not happy years for me. By contrast, my years of
teaching by cooperative learning were the happiest years of my teaching
life. That was a joyous time. In fact, when I asked the cooperative learning students to tell the class what they had found in their shoreline hazard assessment problem, a request that had never drawn much response
as a homework problem in lecture classes, and when the cooperative
learning class then responded enthusiastically, I fully believe that I experienced one of Maslow's (1971) "peak experiences"; in other words, the
most ecstatic moment of my teaching life.

Do you eagerly look forward to your class period, athirst for it to
begin, still excited after it's over? If not, why do you settle for a middling
experience? Teaching is a part of your life. Does your class bring you joy?
Or, in Palmer's (1998) word, "gladness" (p. 30)? If not, why do you settle for receiving less than joy or gladness in what you do? How much better life is when we are excited and joyful in our work! Why hide your gift
for teaching? Why not discover the gift you have for teaching and select
the appropriate teaching technique to reveal it? That technique probably
won't be the one I used. You will find your techniques. It's up to you. But
remember, good teaching is more than techniques (Bain, 2004;
Brookfield, 1995), an admonition that Palmer (1998) sums up this way:
"Good teaching cannot be reduced to technique; good teaching comes
from the identity and integrity of the teacher" (p. 10).

Reflective Questions

- *How will you forgo the "familiar excuses"?*

- *What do you think is the basis for each characteristic of good teaching listed in Table 11.1?*

- *What have you done to motivate and mentor students?*

- *How much pleasure, enjoyment, gladness do you receive from teaching?*

- *What are some of the things that you think the teacher within has said to you?*

CONCLUSION

Well, there you have it. The story of how I changed the way I taught a course, with emphasis on the critical first days. As I said at the beginning, the purpose of this book is not to encourage you to repeat all the steps I took in making the change. Heaven forbid! The references I cite, particularly the headings in the citations, will provide you directions to eliminate many of the steps that I took. Eliminating missteps and not reinventing the wheel are improvements in efficiency. But if we accept the concept that we undergo a process of development as teachers, as mentioned in the last chapter, then attempting to skip a stage in development is not an attempt at efficiency but a guarantee of frustration and disappointment, as with shortcutting stages of any process of growth and development (Covey, 1990). I am not suggesting you take that kind of shortcut.

Not only is your stage of development as a teacher an important consideration as you change your teaching, but so is the type of course you teach. Bear in mind that my course was a senior course with a class of 20 to 35 students. (At the University of Washington, the average class size of upper-division lecture courses over an eight-year period was 30 to 32; for lower-division courses the average was 55 to 59 [Office of Institutional Studies, 2004].) Although some students in my class each year were juniors, most were seniors; most students were women; very few were members of ethnic or racial minorities. The more your course differs from mine in size, number of students, maturity of the students, and diversity of the students, the more the details of your approach will differ from mine.

The purpose of this book is not to urge you to adopt the method of teaching I used, either. "Adapt," as the advice goes, "don't adopt." Far more sources of guidance on teaching and learning, both in general and in your discipline, are available to help you change than were available to help me. By drawing guidance from those sources and applying it to the particular circumstance of your course, and by remembering the context of change described in this book and keeping the end in mind, you can change your course to enhance your students' learning. The purpose of this book is to help you visualize what your course could be like for you and your students during the change.

As you prepare to change the way you teach, there are seven themes of this book that may be of comfort to you at various times during the setup and running of your new "experiment" in teaching.

Accept Risk

Yes, indeed, risk accompanies any change we make from the comfortable and familiar, but we are accomplished risk-takers, both as successful professional researchers and as living human beings. Therefore, taking risks is nothing new for us. We just have to break away from our comfortable habit of teaching, a habit, by the way, that we did not take up voluntarily. We backed into it unwittingly because it was the way we either assumed—or were told—we ought to follow, it was the way of our peers, and it was the way we had experienced from the receiving end as students. It's comfortable, yes, but is it gratifying? Does it fill you with joy or gladness?

By stepping from behind the lectern and walking among your students, you will be more vulnerable, to be sure. The more vulnerable we are, the more risks await us. We can accept those risks, perhaps with difficulty at first, but with greater confidence over time, for the voice of the teacher within will reassure us when what we are doing is right for us. To be doing what we believe to be right increases our self-confidence and minimizes the threat of the risks.

We are not the only one threatened by the risks of our change. As with any change in a process, those people who did not initiate the change may resist it because of the risks it entails for them, at least in the beginning. Students may resist the change for many reasons, some valid, such as the risk they perceive to their success under the old way, some invalid, such as their increased responsibility for their own learning. Your fidelity to the new paradigm and your accomplished persuasiveness, honed in your research arguments, should persuade most of your students to accept the change and convince at least some of them that it enhances their learning. Colleagues may resist it, too. Discretion and humility may be required to deal as successfully with your colleagues in teaching as in research. If so, the skill required is not new. You already know how to use it.

As you gain experience in your new way of teaching, the risks will be transformed into challenges. Oh, there will be things you attempt that fail to achieve what you wish, but by then you will know that teaching under the new paradigm requires continual adaptation. No longer will you be concerned that the failure to meet a learning goal with a technique, activity, or reading might make you look foolish in front of your class. You and the students will accept your teaching as now being in a state of continual improvement. All in all, the risks you will face, though real, are not so threatening as before because you will know why you are facing them and what you hope to accomplish. Even the small accomplishments will feel good because you will believe that you are doing what is right for you and for your students.

Use Feedback

Feedback connects us with our students. We provide them feedback on the status of their learning; they provide us feedback on the status of our teaching. The more nearly instant the feedback in either direction, the better the learning or teaching experience because the quicker the feedback, the sooner the corrections can be made to enhance learning or improve teaching. Waiting until you have finished teaching a topic or the students have finished studying (learning?) a topic before asking for and providing feedback will derogate from the value of the feedback information because no corrections will be possible for the benefit of the students then in the class. Corrections promised for the next time the course is taught are easily—even though unintentionally—forgotten.

The critical step in giving feedback to students will be to make time for discovering how well they are learning what you want them to learn. It will be very easy to discard that activity as an impediment to "covering the material," the old bugaboo. You can guard against the tendency to discard it by remembering that now you are partners with the students in their learning, not that you think you can learn it for them, you can't. But your timely feedback will help them learn in a nonthreatening manner. Timeliness is the key, and there are many methods for doing this without spending hours grading each interaction with the students. Nothing you can do for the students will better demonstrate that you truly care about them and are helping them learn in your class than your providing them timely, and always constructive, feedback on their learning.

The critical step in receiving feedback from students is summoning the courage to ask for it. Now that your goals for teaching will be to help students learn, you will want to achieve those goals and you will want your students to achieve the learning goals you set for them. Any advice you can obtain to help you achieve those goals more effectively, more efficiently, more efficaciously will be a boon not to be spurned. Besides, when you are teaching in a way that feels right to you, you will want to be the best you can be—because it feels so good. It can bring you joy. Feedback from our students is precious, thorns and all.

Reflect

When our interaction with the students in the classroom is such that we know the students are learning; when our feedback to them encourages their learning; when their feedback to us suggests ways in which we can enhance their learning; when we have sources for advice and guidance for improving our teaching; when the experience of being with the students in the classroom is exciting, enjoyable, and intellectually invigorating, it is natural for us to ask, why are we so fortunate? We seek the answer in reflection on our teaching and ourselves. But when we are taking our first uncertain, and possibly uncommitted, steps in changing our teaching, reflection can seem an affectation. Before we can reflect on what underlies our teaching, we have to discover what it is that underlies our teaching, and that can be a challenge if we have never before attempted the discovery.

Reflection is nothing new for us, however. It only seems new when mentioned with respect to our teaching. In our research, we continually reflect on the research problem, the assumptions, the conditions, the methods, the reasoning, all the facets of the research problem and its solution. And we challenge our assumptions, verify the conditions, alter our methods, and so forth, all in the name of improving our ability to achieve our goal—which is to solve the research problem. Our ability to reflect on what we do is proven by the success of our research accomplishments in our discipline, and our reflection is as capable as the research is successful.

The challenge you face is to focus that capability on the assumptions, conditions, methods, reasoning, and other facets of your teaching, and that requires you to identify those assumptions, conditions, methods, and reasoning, possibly for the first time. Now that there is a need for you to reflect, that need itself can provide you with the motivation to succeed.

Adapt and Be Flexible

It should be obvious that changing the way you teach will require you to adapt and be flexible, and that teaching with active learning will require you to continue to adapt and be flexible. Adaptation and flexibility will become a way of life for you as an instructor. One form of adaptation will be your use of instructional technology. I have not discussed this technology, although you have read how I made use of it, because the technology changes too rapidly for a discussion here to be current for long. Your choice of technology, however, should always be based on sound pedagogical principles, just as your choice of research technology is based on sound research principles.

Although this requirement of adaptation and flexibility is indeed foreign to teaching in a highly structured lecture, it is not all that different from our research experience in our discipline. Which of your experiments, first proposed measurements, planned observations, or hypotheses to be tested did you carry through to completion without making some adaptation or exhibiting some flexibility?

We know very well how to adapt, how to think and act with flexibility, because that is our way of dealing successfully with the unexpected. It is a part of our creativity, our "tolerance for ambiguous circumstances" (Shekerjian, 1990). To walk into the site of our research inquiry, direct the inquiry, and walk out again in the structured manner of walking into a lecture hall, delivering a "conclusion-oriented" lecture (McKeachie, 2002), and walking out, and, as in the latter instance, to have only an assumption to satisfy us that our actions produced the results we intended would be unthinkable, for we could not be certain that our action had indeed attained the intended research results, nor would we be responding to the unexpected in either instance.

You will be able to adapt in your teaching because you will give to and take feedback from the students, just as you adapt in your research because you receive feedback from your research activity—your measurement, question, observation, reasoning, colleagues, and so forth. You will detect whether the students are not learning and then adapt to ensure, as best you can, that they do learn. And as the students change from year to year in various characteristics, you can adapt to them. You can present the information you want them to learn in different ways, ways that are appropriate to different student cultural and social backgrounds, individual experiences, or previous knowledge. And the unmentioned part of this adaptation is that the students will learn to adapt, too. Together with the students, you will form a partnership in learning.

Establish a Partnership

As faculty, we have long accepted the total responsibility for the success of our course because the success was measured by the amount of information we delivered to the students over the term, and we easily controlled that delivery. But now, through the feedback you will share with the students on their learning and your teaching, you will be able to share with the students all but the ultimate responsibility for the success of the course. The ultimate responsibility shall always be yours alone, for you will decide how much responsibility, or power, to share.

Although this sharing of responsibility, and with it your loss of complete control of the classroom, does indeed raise a risk for both the students and you, you can be confident of your ability to accept risks, and you can provide students with a scaffolding to help them accept risks. So risks will not deter you and should not deter the students. Besides, the sharing provides the students with a certain level of ownership of the course. And all of us tend to be more interested in what we own a share of than in what we only use.

The students' increased interest in the course will encourage them to contribute suggestions, recommendations, even corrections, to your syllabus or lesson plans that can enhance their learning in the course. This voluntary feedback should be gratefully considered by you and reflected upon for adaptations to enhance their learning. To make the changes that you can and to explain to the students why you cannot make the changes you can't will validate their effort to provide you with feedback and will strengthen your partnership.

Take heart from this conclusion of a study by Bain (2004) of 63 faculty who were identified as excellent college teachers:

> I cannot stress enough the simple yet powerful notion
> that the key to understanding the best teaching can be
> found not in particular practices or rules but in the
> *attitudes* of the teachers, in their *faith* in their students'
> abilities to achieve, in their *willingness* to take their stu-
> dents seriously and to let them assume control of their

own education, and in their *commitment* to let all poli-
cies and practices flow from central learning objectives
and from a mutual respect and agreement between students and teachers. (pp. 78–79)

Accept That You Are Teaching in a Different World

Make no mistake about it: When you teach under the learning-centered
paradigm, you will be teaching in a different world from what you have
been accustomed to. For a while you will be able to remember the old
world, the old paradigm, the old woman in the visual illusion of Figure
10.1 with her downcast face, gathered shawl, and simple cap, but over
time all you will come to see is the new world, the new paradigm, the
young woman with her gracefully turned head, smooth cheek and neck,
and elegant hat and coat. In that new world you will welcome classroom
risks, for they are the challenges that can bring you closer to your goal of
helping your students learn. Feedback and reflection will become second
nature to you, as in your disciplinary research today. And your partnership with your students will also become a natural relationship.

Through your understanding of the difficulty in entering and accepting a different world of practice, you will forgive your own resistance
while trying to make the change in your teaching. And you will understand the resistance to your change that will be exhibited by some of your
students and colleagues, and you will respond to them, or not, with that
understanding. You may choose to inform your colleagues about what
you are doing and you may choose to let your students inform them, or
your own career interest may dictate that you keep your different world
to yourself and your students. And you will eventually realize that some
of your colleagues will never advance in their development as a teacher to
the point of leaving the paradigm they began with. Acquainting them
with the joy you garner from your changed teaching would be pointless,
possibly even misinterpreted to your disadvantage. But that will not
lessen your joy.

Welcome the Joy

Our research in our discipline is exciting and fulfilling. And, yes, it is hard work. But we forget the difficulties when we thrill to finally stating the problem in such a way that it can be solved, when we reason the solution, when the analysis works, and when the synthesis holds firm. What a joyous feeling! Joy—and fatigue! The change in your teaching will enable you to transfer that joy of accomplishment to your classroom, for there will be an external validation of that accomplishment. When your desired accomplishment was to present content, your accomplishment was judged solely by you on the amount of material you covered. That is a small joy, for the risk to success was small because no one but you knew how much content you intended to cover. An accomplishment too small to be shared educes small joy.

But when your desired accomplishment is to enable the students to learn what you want them to learn and to use that learning, your accomplishment is judged not by you alone, but by the feedback between you and your students and your reflection and adaptation in response. Although you no longer fully control the classroom, you now control the joint accomplishment of you, the teacher, and your students, the learners. When the voice of the teacher within tells you that what you are doing is right for you—and for your students—your joy, enthusiasm, and excitement will be infectious. The students will catch it. It will energize your partnership. It will spark the feedback.

The students will become your ambassadors to other classes, telling other students of their experience in your class, asking more questions of their lecturing instructors than any other group of students has before, being told by an instructor not to ask so many questions because he cannot cover all the material if they do—and they will delight in dropping by your office to tell you so. They have truly become active learners, and isn't that your goal for them?

You can share the joy with them. You can change. It's up to you, for, as Marilyn Ferguson observed, "No one can persuade another to change. Each of us guards a gate of change that can only be opened from the inside. We cannot open the gate of another, either by argument or emotional appeal" (as cited in Covey, 1990, pp. 60–61). I have tried to tell you what I found when I opened my gate—what personal joy and gladness, educational success, and professional esteem it brought me, in spite of my stumbles and mistakes. I wish you no less.

APPENDIX

A SKETCH OF THE NATIONAL REFORM OF UNDERGRADUATE EDUCATION

An urge to reform education is like a recurring itch. The current itch in undergraduate education is often dated from the 1960s, when college campuses were overtaken by turmoil that brought to light "the inadequacies and inequalities in American higher education" (Smith, 2002, p. 12). Although some improvements in undergraduate education resulted from recommendations of the various commissions appointed by the federal government and private foundations in the 1970s, such as the establishment of the Fund for the Improvement of Postsecondary Education (FIPSE) in the U.S. Department of Health, Education, and Welfare, education problems persisted, particularly in primary and secondary schools, where the deteriorating performance of students sparked an outcry by parents, the news media, and finally the government. A commission appointed by the U.S. Secretary of Education to examine the problem with primary and secondary education found that "the educational foundations of our society are presently being eroded by a rising tide of mediocrity that threatens our very future as a Nation and a people" (National Commission on Excellence in Education, 1983). Now there's an itch worthy of prolonged scratching. No wonder this report caught the public's attention.

And so in the 1980s educators from primary grades to undergraduate years began asking questions—about how the devil do students learn, about which teaching practices do work to help students learn, about what kind of preparation do teachers need so that they can help students learn better. Quite a few reports were published on research findings, on compendia of good practice in education, and particularly on the need for the assessment of student learning.

For undergraduate education, perhaps the best-known compendium of good practice is the Seven Principles for Good Practice in Undergraduate Education (Chickering & Gamson, 1987). According to these principles, good practice 1) encourages student-faculty contact, 2) encourages cooperation among students, 3) encourages active learning, 4) gives prompt feedback, 5) emphasizes time on task, 6) communicates high expectations, and 7) respects diverse talents and ways of learning. These principles frame a practice far different from the traditional practice of lecturing to passive students who take notes and whose learning is assessed by what they can memorize for a test.

Good practice tended to manifest the principles of learning then being identified, such as 1) students often do not understand as much of the information presented as the instructor thinks; 2) learning involves connecting new information to the students' existing knowledge, which the student might have to restructure; 3) most students learn to understand abstract ideas by beginning with concrete examples; 4) students learn skills such as critical thinking or communicating ideas by practicing them over and over in different contexts; 5) students learn best when they receive prompt feedback and have the opportunity to try again; and 6) students' performance is affected by expectations for that performance (American Association for the Advancement of Science [AAAS] Project 2061, 1990). No wonder most undergraduate faculty who read these principles ignored them. What these principles demanded of them for making a change in classroom teaching simply overwhelmed them. Yet the reform persisted.

In the 1990s, innovation in undergraduate education increased, although not to the extent in primary and secondary education. Some of the innovations were presented across disciplines, as with initiatives of the American Association for Higher Education and the Association of American Colleges and Universities. By 1995, a commission that became known as the Boyer Commission on Educating Undergraduates in the Research University was established. Its 1998 report challenged the research universities to reinvent their undergraduate education programs.

At the same time, the principles of learning were becoming better understood. A National Research Council review of developments in the science of learning, *How People Learn* by Bransford, Brown, and Cocking (1999), is an excellent summary both of how people learn and how teachers can make use of this information to enhance student learning. One of the important points made is that each discipline has its own challenges for learning and teaching, owing to the nature of the subject matter and the procedures used in the discipline. Consequently, much of how we teach, as well as what we teach, is discipline specific. It was natural, then, that disciplines began setting new expectations for their undergraduate education. In science, for example, those expectations were assembled in reports from the National Research Council ([NRC] 1996a) and the National Science Foundation (1996), among other organizations, and continued to be emphasized throughout the decade (NRC, 1999).

Millions of dollars have flowed into innovations in undergraduate education. The funding has come both from private foundations, such as the Kellogg Foundation, Mellon Foundation, and Pew Charitable Trusts in education and the Howard Hughes Medical Institute in science education, and from government agencies, such as the U.S. Department of Education's FIPSE and the National Science Foundation.

By the beginning of the new century, undergraduate education was improving, but not so much as had been hoped. The Boyer Commission's (2002) second report lamented that "many faculty do not yet give teaching a high priority despite administrative efforts" (p. 24). The report of a survey by the Kellogg Commission on the Future of State and Land-Grant Universities (Byrne, 2000) also reported some faculty resistance to reform. A thorough review of education research (Gardiner, 1998) concluded that

> the college experience for most students comprises a
> loosely organized, unfocused curriculum, with unde-
> fined outcomes, classes that emphasize passive learning,
> lectures that transmit low-level information, and assess-
> ments of learning that frequently demand only the
> recall of memorized material or low-level comprehen-
> sion of concepts. (p. 71)

No wonder the vice president of the American Association for Higher Education could conclude in 2000 that the changes in undergraduate education had hardly been revolutionary (Marchese, 2000). The editor of *Science* magazine opined in 2001 (Kennedy, 2001) that "undergraduate science education gets a pass but doesn't earn credit." And resistance will continue, particularly at research universities; see, for example, the discussion by Handelsman et al. (2004) of science faculty resistance at research universities. And just as certainly innovation will continue; see, for example, the survey results by Bain (2004) that "found no great teachers who relied solely on lectures, not even the highly gifted ones" (p. 107) and the report by Halpern and Hakel (2003) on the effort by experts in the learning sciences to inform those in higher education on how to apply the research results on human learning to education.

Enhancing student learning is now a goal of various types of faculty programs. For example, graduate students at many institutions are being prepared for this goal as the next faculty by the Preparing Future Faculty Program, a partnership between the Council of Graduate Schools and the Association of American Colleges and Universities (http://www.preparing-faculty.org/). Several universities provide orientation and training for new faculty through programs such as the Faculty Fellows Program at the University of Washington (http://www.washington.edu/oue/academy/facfellows.html). And an increasing number of universities are providing teaching assistance to existing faculty. (See the teaching/learning centers at many colleges and universities as listed on the web site of the University of Kansas Center for Teaching Excellence: http://www.ku.edu/~cte/resources/websites.html.) In fact, the development of a scholarship of teaching and learning under the guidance of the Carnegie Foundation for the Advancement of Teaching (http://www.carnegiefoundation.org/CASTL/index.htm) is leading to the creation of academies of teaching and learning for faculty at a growing number of institutions. And research on undergraduate education is being recognized on campus by the creation of academic structures such as the Institute for Transforming Undergraduate Education at the University of Delaware (http://www.udel.edu/inst/) and the Reinvention Center (for undergraduate education in research universities) at Stony Brook University (http://www.sunysb.edu/Reinventioncenter/). Perhaps most significant, however, faculty are actually talking about teaching and learning, and more of them are talking and in more forums than "campus opinions" would have us believe (Hutchings, 2004).

Many of the basic ideas in this reform of education are not new. In the early part of the 20th century, educators such as John Dewey and

Alfred North Whitehead were promoting, among other ideas, the importance of having students undertake inquiry in order to learn a subject. And we can trace that idea back through previous centuries. In the 18th century, Jean-Jacques Rousseau stressed learning-by-doing in his book of educational ideas, *Émile* (1762/1989). He wrote about the instructor that "he must not give precepts, he must let the scholar find them out for himself" (p. 19). In the previous century, René Descartes strongly advised, in his *Discourse on Method* (1637/1994), that "one cannot so well seize a thing and make it one's own, when it has been learned from another, as when one has himself discovered it" (p. 51).

Today we speak of learning science by inquiry as the major method for students to use in learning for understanding (AAAS, 1993; NRC, 1996b). The main difference between the promotion of these ideas now, in the early 21st century, and previously is not only the availability of knowledge from research on how people learn but the very breadth of the current reform, both across disciplines and across education levels from kindergarten to graduate school. The reform presses onward.

BIBLIOGRAPHY

Adler, M. J., & Van Doren, C. (1972). *How to read a book* (Rev. ed.). New York, NY: Touchstone.

Albom, M. (1997). *Tuesdays with Morrie: An old man, a young man, and life's greatest lesson.* New York, NY: Doubleday.

American Association for the Advancement of Science Project 2061. (1990). *Science for all Americans.* New York, NY: Oxford University Press.
 - historical perspective - effectiy

American Association for the Advancement of Science Project 2061. (1993). *Benchmarks for science literacy.* New York, NY: Oxford University Press.

American Council on Education. (2003). *Minorities in higher education 2002–2003: Twentieth annual status report.* Washington, DC: Author.

Angelo, T. A., & Cross, K. P. (1993). *Classroom assessment techniques: A handbook for college teachers* (2nd ed.). San Francisco, CA: Jossey-Bass.

Aronson, E. (2000). *Jigsaw classroom.* Retrieved September 26, 2004, from http://www.jigsaw.org/index.html

Aronson, E., Blaney, N., Stephan, C., Sikes, J., & Snapp, M. (1978). *The jigsaw classroom.* Beverly Hills, CA: Sage.

Astin, A. W. (1993). *What matters in college? Four critical years revisited.* San Francisco, CA: Jossey-Bass.

Bain, K. (2004). *What the best college teachers do.* Cambridge, MA: Harvard University Press.

Barnes, C. P. (1994). Questioning in college classrooms. In K. A. Feldman & M. B. Paulsen (Eds.), *Teaching and learning in the college classroom* (pp. 393–409). Needham Heights, MA: Ginn Press.

Barr, R. B., & Tagg, J. (1995, November/December). From teaching to learning—a new paradigm for undergraduate education. *Change, 27*(6), 12–25.

Biggs, J. (1999). What the student does: Teaching for enhanced learning. *Higher Education Research and Development, 18*(1), 57–75.

Boyer Commission on Educating Undergraduates in the Research University. (1998). *Reinventing undergraduate education: A blueprint for America's research universities.* Retrieved July 7, 2004, from the Stony Brook University web site: http://naples.cc.sunysb.edu/Pres/boyer.nsf

Boyer Commission on Educating Undergraduates in the Research University. (2002). *Reinventing undergraduate education: Three years after the Boyer Report.* Retrieved July 7, 2004, from the Stony Brook University web site: http://www.sunysb.edu/pres/0210066-Boyer%20Report%20Final.pdf

Boyer, E. L. (1990). *Scholarship reconsidered: Priorities of the professoriate.* San Francisco, CA: Jossey-Bass.

Bransford, J. D., Brown, A. L., & Cocking, R. R. (Eds.). (1999). *How people learn: Brain, mind, experience, and school.* Washington, DC: National Academy Press.

Brookfield, S. D. (1995). *Becoming a critically reflective teacher.* San Francisco, CA: Jossey-Bass.

Brown, J. S., & Duguid, P. (2000). *The social life of information.* Boston, MA: Harvard Business School Press.

Brown, N. W. (2000). *Creating high performance classroom groups.* New York, NY: Falmer Press.

Byrne, J. V. (2000). *Public higher education reform: 2000: The results of a post–Kellogg Commission survey.* Retrieved July 7, 2004, from the National Association of State Universities and Land-Grant Colleges web site: http://www.nasulgc.org/Kellogg/Kellogg2000_PostComm_survey_summary.pdf

Center for Instructional Development and Research. (2004a). *Inclusive teaching.* Retrieved August 4, 2004, from the University of Washington, Center for Instructional Development and Research web site: http://depts.washington.edu/cidrweb/inclusive/consider.html

Center for Instructional Development and Research. (2004b). *Midterm class interviews (also known as the SGID).* Retrieved April 15, 2004, from the University of Washington, Center for Instructional Development and Research web site: http://depts.washington.edu/cidrweb/SGID.html

Center for Research on Learning and Teaching. (2004). *Multicultural teaching.* Retrieved August 4, 2004, from the University of Michigan, Center for Research on Learning and Teaching web site: http://www.crlt.umich.edu/multiteaching/multiteaching.html

Center for Teaching. (1999). *Teaching Goals Inventory . . . online!* Retrieved March 8, 2004, from the University of Iowa, Center for Teaching web site: http://www.uiowa.edu/~centeach/tgi/index.html

Center for Teaching Excellence. (n.d.). *Active learning.* Retrieved September 3, 2004, from the University of Medicine and Dentistry of New Jersey, Center for Teaching Excellence web site: http://www.umdnj.edu/meg/active_general.htm

ChemConnections. (n.d.). *Synopsis of ChemConnections evaluation studies.* Retrieved September 7, 2004, from the University of California–Berkeley, ChemConnections web site: http://mc2.cchem.berkeley.edu/Evaluation/ChCxn%20evals%20syn-Final.html

Chickering, A. W., & Gamson, Z. F. (1987, March). Seven principles for good practice in undergraduate education. *AAHE Bulletin, 39*(7), 3–7. Retrieved March 16, 2004, from http://aahebulletin.com/public/ archive/sevenprinciples1987.asp

Chism, N. V. N. (1999). *Peer review of teaching: A sourcebook.* Bolton, MA: Anker.

Christensen, C. R. (1991). The discussion teacher in action: Questioning, listening, and response. In C. R. Christensen, D. A. Garvin, & A. Sweet (Eds.), *Education for judgment: The artistry of discussion leadership* (pp. 153–172). Boston, MA: Harvard Business School Press.

Clarke, J. (1994). Pieces of the puzzle: The jigsaw method. In S. Sharan (Ed.), *Handbook of cooperative learning methods* (pp. 34–50). Westport, CT: Greenwood Press.

Cooperative Learning Center. (n.d.). *What is cooperative learning?* Retrieved September 3, 2004, from the University of Minnesota, Cooperative Learning Center web site: http://www.co-operation.org/

Covey, S. R. (1990). *The 7 habits of highly effective people.* New York, NY: Fireside.

Cross, K. P. (1977). Not *can,* but *will* college teaching be improved? In J. A. Centra (Ed.), *New directions for higher education: No. 17. Renewing and evaluating teaching* (pp. 1–15). San Francisco, CA: Jossey-Bass.

Cross, K. P., & Steadman, M. H. (1996). *Classroom research: Implementing the scholarship of learning.* San Francisco, CA: Jossey-Bass.

Davis, B. G. (1993). *Tools for teaching.* San Francisco, CA: Jossey-Bass.

Davis, B. G., Wood, L., & Wilson, R. C. (1983). Suggestion 99: Periodically borrow students' lecture notes. In *A Berkeley compendium of suggestions for teaching with excellence* [Section 13]. Retrieved March 30, 2004, from http://teaching.berkeley.edu/compendium/suggestions/file99.html

Derek Bok Center for Teaching and Learning. (2002–2004). *Tips for teachers: Teaching in racially diverse college classrooms.* Retrieved August 4, 2004, from the Harvard University, Derek Bok Center for Teaching and Learning web site: http://bokcenter.fas.harvard.edu/docs/TFTrace.html

Descartes, R. (1994). *Discourse on method* (J. Veitch, Trans.). London, England: J. M. Dent & Sons, Everyman's Library. (Original work published 1637)

Duch, B. J., Groh, S. E., & Allen, D. E. (2001). *The power of problem-based learning.* Sterling, VA: Stylus.

Eble, K. E. (1983). *The aims of college teaching.* San Francisco, CA: Jossey-Bass.

Eble, K. E. (1988). *The craft of teaching* (2nd ed.). San Francisco, CA: Jossey-Bass.

Erwin, T. D. (1991). *Assessing student learning and development: A guide to the principles, goals, and methods of determining college outcomes.* San Francisco, CA: Jossey-Bass.

Faculty Teaching Excellence Program. (2004). *Teaching and learning series on diversity.* Retrieved November 14, 2004, from the University of Colorado, Faculty Teaching Excellence Program web site: http://www.colorado.edu/ftep/diversity/index.html

Fink, L. D. (2003). *Creating significant learning experiences: An integrated approach to designing college courses.* San Francisco, CA: Jossey-Bass.

Finkel, D. L. (2000). *Teaching with your mouth shut.* Portsmouth, NH: Heinemann.

Gardiner, L. F. (1998). Why we must change: The research evidence. *Thought and Action, 14*(1), 71–88.

Garvin, D. A. (1991). Barriers and gateways to learning. In C. R. Christensen, D. A. Garvin, & A. Sweet (Eds.), *Education for judgment: The artistry of discussion leadership* (pp. 3–13). Boston, MA: Harvard Business School Press.

Gibbs, G., Haigh, M., & Lucas, L. (1996). Class size, coursework assessment and student performance in geography: 1984–94. *Journal of Geography in Higher Education, 20*(2), 181–192.

Grunert, J. (1997). *The course syllabus: A learning-centered approach.* Bolton, MA: Anker.

Halpern, D. F., & Hakel, M. D. (2003, July/August). Applying the science of learning to the university and beyond. *Change, 35*(4), 36–41.

Handelsman, J., Ebert-May, D., Beichner, R., Bruns, P., Chang, A., DeHaan, R., et al. (2004, April 23). Scientific teaching. *Science, 304*(5670), 521–522.

Hebert, F., & Loy, M. (2002). The evolution of a teacher-professor: Applying behavior change theory to faculty development. In D. Lieberman & C. Wehlburg (Eds.), *To improve the academy: Vol. 20. Resources for faculty, instructional, and organizational development* (pp. 197–207). Bolton, MA: Anker.

Hord, S. M., Rutherford, W. L., Huling-Austin, L., & Hall, G. E. (1987). *Taking charge of change.* Austin, TX: Southwest Educational Development Laboratory.

Housel, E. S., Huston, A. L., Martin, C. A., & Pierce, T. L. (1995). Student perspectives on a cooperative-learning experience. *Journal of Geological Education, 43,* 330–331.

Huff, C. (1998). *An invitation to psychology.* Paper presented at the Fall Mellby Lecture at St. Olaf College. Retrieved May 1, 2004, from http://www.stolaf.edu/people/huff/prose/mellby.html

Hutchings, P. (1990, June). *Assessment and the way it works.* Paper presented at the fifth annual American Association for Higher Education Conference on Assessment, Washington, DC.

Hutchings, P. (1996). *Making teaching community property: A menu for peer collaboration and peer review.* Washington, DC: American Association for Higher Education.

Hutchings, P. (Ed.). (1998). *The course portfolio: How faculty can examine their teaching to advance practice and improve student learning.* Washington, DC: American Association for Higher Education.

Hutchings, P. (2004, January). Building a better conversation about learning. *Carnegie Perspectives.* Retrieved July 26, 2004, from http://www .carnegiefoundation.org/perspectives/perspectives2004.Jan.htm

Jersild, A. T. (1955). *When teachers face themselves.* New York, NY: Columbia University, Teachers College, Bureau of Publications.

Johnson, D. W., Johnson, R. T., & Smith, K. A. (1991). *Active learning: Cooperation in the college classroom.* Edina, MN: Interaction Books.

Johnson, D. W., Johnson, R. T., & Stanne, M. B. (2000). *Cooperative learning methods: A meta-analysis.* Retrieved September 7, 2004, from the University of Minnesota, Cooperative Learning Center web site: http:// www.co-operation.org/pages/cl-methods.html

Johnson, S. (1998). *Who moved my cheese? An a-mazing way to deal with change in your work and in your life.* New York, NY: G. P. Putnam's Sons.

Kemble, E. C., & Birch, F. (1970). Percy Williams Bridgman, April 21, 1882–August 20, 1961. *Biographical Memoirs, National Academy of Sciences, 41,* 23–67.

Kennedy, D. (2001, August 31). College science: Pass, no credit [Editorial]. *Science, 293*(5535), 1557.

Klein, G. (1998). *Sources of power: How people make decisions.* Cambridge, MA: MIT Press.

Kraft, R. G. (2002). Teaching excellence and the inner life of a faculty. In S. M. Intrator (Ed.), *Stories of the courage to teach: Honoring the teacher's heart* (pp. 203–217). San Francisco, CA: Jossey-Bass.

Kuhn, T. S. (1996). *The structure of scientific revolutions* (3rd ed.). Chicago, IL: University of Chicago Press.

Lawrence, G. (1982). *People types & tiger stripes: A practical guide to learning styles* (2nd ed.). Gainesville, FL: Center for Application of Psychological Types.

Lowman, J. (1995). *Mastering the techniques of teaching* (2nd ed.). San Francisco, CA: Jossey-Bass.

Marchese, T. (2000, May/June). Undergraduate reform [Editorial]. *Change, 32*(3), 4.

Maslow, A. H. (1971). *The farther reaches of human nature.* New York, NY: Viking.

Mazur, E. (1997). *Peer instruction: A user's guide.* Upper Saddle River, NJ: Prentice Hall.

McConnell, D. A., Steer, D. N., & Owens, K. A. (2003). Assessment and active learning strategies for introductory geology courses. *Journal of Geoscience Education, 51*(2), 205–216.

McDermott, L. C., Shaffer, P. S., & the Physics Education Group at the University of Washington. (1998). *Tutorials in introductory physics.* Upper Saddle River, NJ: Prentice Hall.

McGuire, S. Y., & Williams, D. A. (2002). The millennial learner: Challenges and opportunities. In D. Lieberman & C. Wehlburg (Eds.), *To improve the academy: Vol. 20. Resources for faculty, instructional, and organizational development* (pp. 185–196). Bolton, MA: Anker.

McKeachie, W. J. (2002). *McKeachie's teaching tips: Strategies, research, and theory for college and university teachers* (11th ed.). Boston, MA: Houghton Mifflin.

McKinney, K. (2004). *Active learning.* Retrieved September 3, 2004, from the Illinois State University, Center for the Advancement of Teaching web site: http://www.cat.ilstu.edu/teaching_tips/handouts/newactive.shtml

McManus, D. A. (1995). Changing a course in marine geology from lecture format to a cooperative-learning format. *Journal of Geological Education, 43*, 327–330.

McManus, D. A. (2001). The two paradigms of education and the peer review of teaching. *Journal of Geoscience Education, 49*(5), 423–434.

Meyers, C., & Jones, T. B. (1993). *Promoting active learning: Strategies for the college classroom.* San Francisco, CA: Jossey-Bass.

Millis, B. J., & Cottell, P. G., Jr. (1998). *Cooperative learning for higher education faculty.* Phoenix, AZ: ACE/Oryx Press.

Murray, K., & MacDonald, R. (1997). The disjunction between lecturers' conceptions of teaching and their claimed educational practice. *Higher Education, 33*(3), 331–349.

National Center for Case Study Teaching in Science. (n.d.). *The case method of teaching science.* Retrieved September 3, 2004, from http://ublib.buffalo.edu/libraries/projects/cases/teaching/teaching.html

National Commission on Excellence in Education. (1983). *A nation at risk: The imperative for educational reform.* Washington, DC: U.S. Department of Education. Retrieved July 7, 2004, from http://www.ed.gov/pubs/NatAtRisk/title.html

National Institute for Science Education. (n.d.). *Field-tested learning assessment guide.* Retrieved September 4, 2004, from http://www.flaguide.org/

National Research Council. (1996a). *From analysis to action: Undergraduate education in science, mathematics, engineering, and technology.* Washington, DC: National Academy Press.

National Research Council. (1996b). *National science education standards.* Washington, DC: National Academy Press.

National Research Council. (1999). *Transforming undergraduate education in science, mathematics, engineering, and technology.* Washington, DC: National Academy Press.

National Research Council. (2000). *Inquiry and the national science education standards: A guide for teaching and learning.* Washington, DC: National Academy Press.

National Research Council. (2001). *Knowing what students know: The science and design of educational assessment.* Washington, DC: National Academy Press.

National Science Board. (2004). *Science and engineering indicators* (NSB 04-01). Arlington, VA: National Science Foundation. Retrieved August 4, 2004, from http://www.nsf.gov/sbe/srs/seind04/start.htm

National Science Foundation. (1996). *Shaping the future: New expectations for undergraduate education in science, mathematics, engineering, and technology* (NSF Publication 96-139). Washington, DC: Author.

National Science Foundation. (2004). *Women, minorities, and persons with disabilities in science and engineering.* Retrieved July 30, 2004, from http://www.nsf.gov/sbe/srs/wmpd/figa-1.htm

Nilson, L. B. (2003). *Teaching at its best: A research-based resource for college instructors* (2nd ed.). Bolton, MA: Anker.

Nyquist, J. D., & Wulff, D. H. (1996). *Working effectively with graduate assistants.* Thousand Oaks, CA: Sage.

Office of Educational Assessment. (1999–2003). *Recent surveys of students and alumni.* Retrieved April 9, 2004, from the University of Washington, Office of Educational Assessment web site: http://www.washington .edu/oea/asessurv.htm

Office of Institutional Studies. (2004). *University of Washington factbook [average class meeting size by course level and instruction types].* Retrieved July 5, 2004, from the University of Washington, Office of Institutional Studies web site: http://www.washington.edu/admin/factbook/

Palmer, P. J. (1998). *The courage to teach: Exploring the inner landscape of a teacher's life.* San Francisco, CA: Jossey-Bass.

Paulson, D. R., & Faust, J. L. (2003). *Active learning for the college classroom.* Retrieved September 3, 2004, from the California State University–Los Angeles, Los Angeles Collaborative for Teacher Excellence web site: http://www.calstatela.edu/dept/chem/chem2/ Active/index.htm

Peer-Led Team Learning. (2004). *Comparing the performance of groups of students with and without PLTL workshops.* Retrieved September 7, 2004, from the City College of New York, Peer-Led Team Learning Workshop Project web site: http://www.sci.ccny.cuny.edu/~chemwksp/ResearchAndEvaluationComparisons.html

Peer Review of Teaching. (2001). *Course portfolio initiative.* Retrieved March 12, 2004, from the Indiana University, Peer Review of Teaching web site: http://www.indiana.edu/~deanfac/portfolio/def.html

Perry, R. P., & Smart, J. C. (Eds.). (1997). *Effective teaching in higher education: Research and practice.* New York, NY: Agathon.

Polanyi, M. (1962). *Personal knowledge: Towards a post-critical philosophy* (Corrected ed.). Chicago, IL: University of Chicago Press.

Prégent, R. (1994). *Charting your course: How to prepare to teach more effectively* (M. Parker, Trans.). Madison, WI: Magna. (Original work published 1990)

Race, P. (2000). *500 tips on group learning.* London, England: Kogan Page.

Race, P. (2001). *The lecturer's toolkit: A practical guide to learning, teaching, & assessment.* London, England: Kogan Page.

Repplier, A. (1971). *Times and tendencies* (Reprint). Freeport, NY: Books for Libraries Press. (Original work published 1931)

Rousseau, J-J. (1989). *Émile* (B. Foxley, Trans.). London, England: J. M. Dent & Sons, Everyman's Library. (Original work published 1762)

Seldin, P. (2004). *The teaching portfolio: A practical guide to improved performance and promotion/tenure decisions* (3rd ed.). Bolton, MA: Anker.

Shekerjian, D. (1990). *Uncommon genius: How great ideas are born.* New York, NY: Penguin.

Shulman, L. S. (1986). Those who understand: Knowledge growth in teaching. *Educational Researcher, 15*(2), 4–14.

Shulman, L. S. (1999, July/August). Taking learning seriously. *Change, 31*(4), 10–17.

Smith, K. A., & Waller, A. A. (1997). Afterword: New paradigms for college teaching. In W. E. Campbell & K. A. Smith (Eds.), *New paradigms for college teaching* (pp. 269–281). Edina, MN: Interaction Book.

Smith, V. (2002, September/October). FIPSE's early years: Seeking innovation and change in higher education. *Change, 34*(5), 10–16.

Stein, R. F., & Hurd, S. (2000). *Using student teams in the classroom: A faculty guide.* Bolton, MA: Anker.

Suskie, L. (2004). *Assessing student learning: A common sense guide.* Bolton, MA: Anker.

Tagg, J. (2003). *The learning paradigm college.* Bolton, MA: Anker.

University of Delaware Problem-Based Learning. (1999). *Problem-based learning.* Retrieved September 3, 2004, from http://www.udel.edu/pbl/

Walvoord, B. E., & Anderson, V. J. (1998). *Effective grading: A tool for learning and assessment.* San Francisco, CA: Jossey-Bass.

Weimer, M. (2002). *Learner-centered teaching.* San Francisco, CA: Jossey-Bass.

Wlodkowski, R. J., & Ginsberg, M. G. (2003). *Diversity and motivation: Culturally responsive teaching.* San Francisco, CA: Jossey-Bass.

INDEX

Headings for entries to the course when taught as lecture and examination are followed by (before the change).

Headings for entries to the course as cooperative learning are followed by (after the change).

Headings for entries to the course in intermediate format (pp. 39–43) are followed by ("special class").

Learning by doing. *See also* Application of
knowledge
a step toward active learning, 34, 36
applying knowledge, 38, 85
made more explicit, 63
trend in my teaching, 38
Learning centers. *See* Teaching centers
Learning-centered paradigm, 142, 144, 145, 172
Learning outcomes, 60, 62, 93–94. *See also*
Goals for course
(after the change), 61, 91–94
(before the change), 36
(in "special class"), 38
Lecture notes, 2, 60
Lecturing
in active learning, 106
best done with adaptability and flexibility,
105–106
conclusion-oriented mode of, 42
effective, 42, 79–80, 81
forestalls student questions, 4
poor technique of, 6, 41
by students in mixed groups, 79–80
training for, not expected, 2, 5. *See also*
Teaching innocently
Loneliness of teaching, 140
Lowman, J., 83
Loy, M., 56, 98
Lucas, L., 102

MacArthur Awards, 27–28
MacDonald, R., 148
Marchese, T., 177
Martin, C. A., 85, 129
Maslow, A. H., 162
Mazur, E., 80, 135
McConnell, D. A., 102
McDermott, L. C., 85
McGuire, S. Y., 146
McKeachie, W. J., xi, 13, 35, 36, 41, 42, 49,
60, 61, 64, 66, 67, 70, 79, 80, 84, 85, 90,
91, 99, 100, 105, 106, 113, 170
McKinney, K., 33
McManus, D. A., 112, 119, 129, 141, (table)
143, 148, (table) 159
Mellon Foundation, 177
Meyers, C., 33, 38, 60, 65, 67, 68, 77, 84,
141, 142, (table) 143, (table) 159

Millis, B. J., 33, 61, 66, 67, 85, 95, 99, 100,
102, 103
Mindset List, The, 146
Minorities. *See also* Diverse student body as
percentage of college-age population, viii, 146
few in science, 42
Minorities in Higher Education, 146
Minority Scientists Network, 147
Misconceptions by students, 135
Mixed groups, 78–81. *See also* Jigsaw
eliminated, 107
formation of, 76
passive note taking in, 78–79
peer tutors in, 80
synthesis preparation by, 80
values of student lecture in, 79–80
Motivating students. *See also* Instructor-student
relationship
and their original motivation, 49
by their natural interests, 92, 109–110
intrinsic versus extrinsic motivation,
84–85, 108
under different paradigms of education
(table), 159
Murray, K., 148

National Association of Geoscience Teachers,
(table) 143, (table) 159
National Center for Case Study Teaching in
Science, 33
National Commission on Excellence in
Education, 175
National Institute for Science Education, 103
National Research Council, 82, 89, 102, 109,
110, 152, 176, 179
National Science Board, 146
National Science Foundation, viii, 82, 110,
146, 177
National Teaching and Learning Forum,
Monthly Conference Calendar of the, 133
Nilson, L. B., 50, 67, 92, 106
Novice learner
characteristics of, 21–22
as cooperative learning instructor, 49, 62,
74, 75, 81
difference from expert learner, 21
at Meeting, 52, 53
Nyquist, J. D., 56, 144

Teaching at research universities
  not discussed by faculty, 50, 55
  improvements in, 156
  secondary responsibility, ix, 2
  share results of, as for research, 124–125
  no rewards for, because no standards for, 156, 157–158
Teaching awards, 37, 158
Teaching, boring. *See* Boring teaching
Teaching-centered paradigm. *See also* Teaching, habit of (before the change)
  as a habit, 158
  most faculty learned under the, 12
  not usually recognized as a paradigm, 141–142
  other assumptions of, 145
  principal assumption of, 143
  weakness of, in research universities, 12
Teaching centers, 48, 128, 178
Teaching Goals Inventory, 26–27, 32, 65, 90
Teaching, good, 156–157, 162
Teaching, habit of (before the change). *See also* Teaching-centered paradigm
  anxiety of, 18
  breaking the, 34, 160, 166
  duty rather than desire, 3, 8, 18
Teaching-centered paradigm as a, 158–160
Teaching, improvement of
  (after the change), 105–120
  (before the change), 10, 105
Teaching, in the discipline, 135–136, 177. *See also* Pedagogical content knowledge
Teaching innocently, 6–9, 62
Teaching log
  contents of, can be kept private, 122–124
  contents of, can be shared, 124–137
  defined, 121
  and hazard of private self-reflection, 123
  summary as preparation for change in teaching, 122, 126
Teaching methods
  different application under different paradigms of education, 149
  move students toward learning outcomes, 60
  usual basis for contrasting paradigms of education, 142
Teaching moment, 36, 99–100
Teaching portfolio, 32, 93

Teaching with Your Mouth Shut, 76
Technology. *See* Instructional technology
Themes of book, 166–174
Time management, for group work versus lecturing, 77

University of Delaware Problem-Based Learning, 33
University of Kansas Center for Teaching Excellence, 178

Van Doren, C., 50

Waller, A. A., 141, 142, (table) 143, (table) 159
Walvoord, B. E., 73, 76, 101
Washington Center for Improving the Quality of Undergraduate Education, The Evergreen State College, 133
Weimer, M., 39, 56, 60, 61, 65, 73, 74, 77, 84, 86, 94, 95, 96, 100, 106, 113, 124, 144, 152
Whitehead, Alfred North, 179
Williams, D. A., 146
Wilson, R. C., 79
Wlodkowski, R. J., 67
Women students
  as ambassadors for innovative teaching, 128, 129, 131
  attracted to class, 117
  comments change class, 46–47, 98
  describe lecture class, 62
  display of trust, 48
  insist I involve more faculty in the change, 139
  most and best students, 42, 165
  volunteer in class, 98
Wood, L., 79
Writing, benefits of non-technical, 96
Wulff, D. H., 56, 144